The Ultimate Quiz Book

FOOTBALL FEVER

The Ultimate Quiz Book

FOOTBALL FEVER

SRINJOY CHOWDHURY

PRABHAT PAPERBACKS

Published by
PRABHAT PAPERBACKS
An imprint of Prabhat Prakashan Pvt. Ltd.
4/19 Asaf Ali Road,
New Delhi-110002 (INDIA)
e-mail: prabhatbooks@gmail.com

ISBN 978-93-5521-437-9
FOOTBALL FEVER
by Srinjoy Chowdhury

Edition
First, 2023

Price
₹ 250 (Rupees Two Hundred Fifty Only)

Printed at
Sanjay Printers, Sahibabad

For Kaushiki Chowdhury

AUTHOR'S NOTE

Football fever isn't just about victory and defeat, about goals scored and chances missed, about delight and despair. It's about football as a slice of life, as an unending international festival.

If Pele and Diego Maradona and Lionel Messi and Cristiano Ronaldo are undoubtedly stars of the book, the supporting cast includes Nobel laureates and world leaders. There's Albert Camus and Fidel Castro, there's Shahrukh Khan and Sylvester Stallone. Football fever is a celebration of the world's favourite sport.

The book aspires to be interactive and is deliberately structured into rounds of eight, the standard format for a live quiz. It's right for a classroom quiz with eight teams of three or four students. The book is ideal for duels between friends. And a reader can dribble through the book: it's an opportunity to laugh as you learn. So, good luck!

CONTENTS

ROUND 1

1. Edson Arantes do Nascimento was once appointed as the minister of sports in his country. How is he better known as?

2. After 55 years of support, this club in 1999 decided to offer Amartya Sen, who was awarded the Nobel Prize in Economics in 1998, life membership for his "constant loyalty." Name the club.

3. After a tattoo on his arm, Diego Maradona, who captained his country to victory in the 1986 World Cup, said that the two greatest sons of Argentina were united in the same body. Who was the other 'great son' tattooed on his arm?

4. One of Nike's advertisement campaigns was based on a famous goal scored in a club game. "What if you asked God to make you the best soccer player in the world? And he was actually listening" was the slogan. Who was the goal scorer?

5. Who said that by studying economics at Columbia University, following U.S. President Barack Obama's re-election campaign and talking with actor-director Woody Allen and former world chess champion Garry Kasparov, he has become a better football strategist?

6. In Karan Johar's film *Kabhi Alvida Naa Kehna*, Shah Rukh Khan acts as Dev Saran, a football player living in New York City. He is forced to give up playing football. Why?

7. This world leader is a football fan. In 2012, he got himself a Los Angeles Galaxy's David Beckham shirt. In 2013, he took a selfie at Manchester City's training arena with Sergio Aguero and David Cameron, then Britain's Prime Minister. Michel Temer, then Brazilian President, presented him with a Brazilian football jersey (a No. 10, which is associated with Pele, Zico and Neymar, with his name on the back.) Who was the leader?

8. After India defeated Taiwan 5-0 in June 2018, an Indian player who had scored a hattrick in the match and was very disappointed with the poor turnout, uploaded a video on Twitter requesting people to attend India's matches. His video went viral and the Indian team played before thousands of people in the next matches. Who was the Indian player?

❑

ROUND 2

9. It is 1973. The Indian football team, still a strong Asian side, is preparing for the prestigious Merdeka tournament. Siddhartha Shankar Ray, then chief minister of Bengal, writes to the authorities, requesting that no footballer from Bengal is included in the side. Why?

10. Spain is one of the world's football giants. In 2022, Spain defended the Women's Under-17 World Championships, defeating their rivals by a solitary goal. Which country did Spain defeat?

11. These countries have been the superstars of football. FIFA began ranking men's national teams in December 1992. In the first 30 years, only eight countries were ranked No. 1. Six of the countries were Argentina, Brazil, France, Germany, Italy and Spain. Name the other two countries.

12. When Cristiano Ronaldo scored his 806th and 807th goals for club and country, he overtook Josef Bican's record of 805, an estimate by FIFA. Bican began playing in the 1930s and continued till the 1950s. He played principally for two countries. Name them.

13. There was a time when India was a football giant and even missed an Olympic bronze in the 1956 Olympic Games in Melbourne. A great coach of that period was Syed Abdul Rahim. Bollywood has recently made a film about Rahim. Who was the actor playing this character in the film?

14. In 2018, a match between these two countries, playing after two decades, was called "The Earth Derby," keeping in mind potential viewership. It ended in a goalless draw. Who were the two countries?

15. Andriy Shevchenko, who played 111 internationals and is now a football manager, launched in 2022, Play Your Part, a campaign to raise money for food, clothing and medicines For whom?

16. Italy, the European football champions in 2021, were eliminated in the World Cup 2022 qualifying round playoff by a goal in the final moments of a match. Alexander Trajkovski scored the last-gasp goal. Who defeated Italy?

❑

ROUND 3

17. In 2021, she was the first footballer to win these awards in the same year: the Ballon d'Or Féminin, the UEFA Women's Player of the Year and the Best FIFA Women's Player. In 2022, she was awarded the Ballon d'Or Féminin again. Who was the player?

18. Pele played 40 international games with this great Brazilian. Of those 40 games, Brazil won 36 and drew four. Not even one was lost. Name Pele's great colleague.

19. This is perhaps one of the greatest successes in inspiring a football team and ensuring national unity. Before the Africa Cup of Nations semi-final, the country's President went into the dressing room of the national team, shook hands with all the players and said: "Boys, I leave the country in your hands." The team won the semi-finals 3-0 against Ghana, the favourites, and in the final, defeated Tunisia 2-0. Identify the President and of course, the national team?

20. Chennaiyin Football Club, part of the Indian Super League, has amongst its owners two celebrities: a cricketer and a Bollywood star. Name them.

21. One of the most exciting Champions League matches was on April 23, 2003, between Real Madrid and Manchester United. This was the second leg of the quarterfinals with Real Madrid 3-1 ahead in the first leg. Manchester United won the see-saw tie 4-3, even if Real Madrid advanced to the semifinals with a 6-5 win. One of the spectators, watching the match at Old Trafford was a very rich man. After the match, he decided to buy a football team. Who was that man?

22. *Bend it Like Beckham* was dubbed into Hindi and called *Football Shootball Hai Rabba—Bend it Like Beckham*. Name the actor who bent it like Beckham?

23. Robert Lewandowski, the Polish striker, has scored over 600 goals playing for club and country. Most, 344 goals of them, were for Bayern Munich. For whom did he score the next highest: 103 goals?

24. There is no place for racism in football and in 2022, after an incident during a match against Tunisia which Brazil won 5-1, a Brazilian player was subjected to abuse. A banana was thrown at him. This was condemned by the CBF or the Brazilian Football Confederation and the team lined up with a banner that said: "Without our black players we wouldn't have stars on our shirts." Name the black player.

❑

ROUND 4

25. Which footballer (104 internationals, 40 goals) founded the Hamro Sikkim Party in 2018? He said he was inspired by the Aam Admi Party and wanted to fight corruption. Appropriately, the party's election symbol was the whistle.

26. Queen Elizabeth reigned from 1952 to 2022—all of 70 years. During her time as monarch, which English club won the maximum number of games in major leagues—the first division in the English football league and then, the Premier League.

27. Antonin Panenka is still celebrated for his European Cup-winning goal for Czechoslovakia against West Germany in 1976. What is a "Panenka?"

28. Steve Hodge, a midfielder, played for England in the mid-80s. In 2022, Sotheby's sold a football-related artefact Hodge had for decades for nearly $US 9.3 million. What was that artefact?

29. The El Clasico is a high-profile match between two Spanish teams, Real Madrid and Barcelona. But a Clasico match in October 2020 was the first of its kind. Barcelona won 4-0. Why was this match, a low-profile one, so special?

30. With West Bengal and Kerala still tied 1-1 after extra-time in the final of the 2022 Santosh Trophy, a tie-breaker was inevitable. Kerala won 5-4 in the tie-breaker with Sanju G., Bibin Ajayan, Jijo Joseph, Jesin T. and Faslu Rahman scoring. For West Bengal, Dilip Orawn, Bablu Oran, Tanmoy Ghosh and Priyant Kumar scored. Who missed?

31. This football club, one of the world's most celebrated, began life as a rowing club in 1895. It played its first official football match only in 1912, over a decade later. It's mascot is of all birds, the vulture. Name the club?

32. This great footballer was often criticised and accused of not giving his best for his national team and much less for his club, Real Madrid. Marca, a Spanish sports newspaper, called him a "parasite." With the remarks was a cartoon of this footballer as a tsetse fly, which causes sleeping sickness, sucking blood from the Real Madrid crest. Name the footballer.

❑

ROUND 5

33. As a schoolboy, Rishi Sunak, appointed as Prime Minister of Britain on 25th October 2022, played cricket, hockey and football, Which football club does he support?

34. What do the following referees have in common: Stephanie Frappart of France, Salima Mukansanga of Rwanda and Yoshimi Yamashita of Japan?

35. "All that I know most surely about morality and obligations I owe to football." This is what a Nobel laureate in Literature once said. He was a goalkeeper for his school and club side, but never did more because of his damaged lungs. Who was that person?

36. In 2011, Arun Roy made a film called *Egaro: the Immortal Eleven*. It was about a major incident in the history of India in the 20th century. What was the incident?

37. This World Cup faced serious challenges. First, Colombia backed out because of financial and political problems. Then, the country that took over was hit by an earthquake months before the tournament was to begin. The official death toll was 5,000, but many more people may have died. Large parts of the capital were flattened, but somehow, the World Cup happened despite criticism about the expenditure at a time thousands desperately needed help. Who was the host country?

38. This superstar footballer acts as Joao, a monk in *Money Heist*, the popular television show. In the show, he advises The Professor and Berlin, two main characters. Who was the footballer?

39. The first Asian nation to reach the semi-finals in the Olympics was India in 1956, in Melbourne, defeating Australia 4-2. The first Asian with a hat-trick in the Olympics was also an Indian. Who was that person?

40. He was one of cricket's greatest all-rounders, but he also played football for Scunthorpe United, an English club. He played 11 matches between 1979 and 1984 in the midfield, mostly at centre-half. Name the cricketer.

❑

ROUND 6

41. From the late 40s, for nearly a decade, the "Pancha Pandavas" ruled over the Maidan in Kolkata. This was the era when teams played with five forwards: The Pandavas were P. Venkatesh (right-wing), Appa Rao (inside-right), K.P. Dhanraj (centre-forward), Ahmed Khan (inside-left) and P.B. Saleh (left-wing). And the club they played for was almost invincible at that time. Name the club.

42. In 2020, this footballer, who has played 97 times for Brazil, was sentenced to five months in prison after he and his brother Roberto de Assis, were found guilty of falsifying passport documents. He could have been in jail for five years, but was in jail in Paraguay for five months and fined $100,000. Name the footballer.

43. The first African team in the World Cup quarter-finals was Cameroon, led by Roger Milla, in 1990. Which African country nearly reached the semi-finals in 2010, and missed out because Asamoah Gyan, the captain, failed to convert a penalty in the dying seconds of the match against Uruguay? Then, Uruguay won the penalty shootout 4-2 and reached the semi-finals.

44. He was abandoned by his parents and grew up in a foster home in Aluva, Kochi. People noticed he could play football. He moved to Bokaro and moved back to Kochi to play in the Kerala Premier League and is one of the state's Santosh Trophy winning side's stars. Who is the person?

45. Barcelona's football academy is La Masia. Which country's soccer school is Aspire Academy, where over half the national side has learnt the game as have virtually all the juniors?

46. It was a great moment for this player, but after an excellent performance, he angrily said: "Today, I needed to win a final for my career, for all the hard work to put respect on my name as I don't think I get enough respect, especially in England. I saw a lot of criticism, even after a great season". This is a great player speaking after winning the Man of the Match award. Who is that player?

47. Marcello Lippi, manager of the World Cup-winning Italian team in 2006 and also, of Juventus and more recently, China, has said this about two rival football personalities in 2022. "They are two mavericks who have made each other better. It's like Lionel Messi and Cristiano Ronaldo...I don't like to talk about them as geniuses. That would be overblown, too grandiloquent. Both are undoubtedly two of the best in their position." Who are the two people?

48. What, in world football, is the Finalissima or Grand Final?

❑

ROUND 7

49. Alia Bhatt, the Bollywood actress, had pinned on the wall in her Mumbai flat a football jersey with "RK (her husband Ranbir Kapoor) at the back. The jersey of which international club?

50. France won the World Cup in 1998 and 2018 and is one of the top international sides. India barely makes it to the top 100. In 1960, however, in the Olympics in Rome, India drew 1-1 with France. Who, one of India's most famous footballers, scored for India?

51. "I just went mental. Honestly, I didn't know what to do. I didn't think about it. I didn't plan it. It was all right, though, weren't it?" This is what a very successful woman footballer said in 2022 after a memorable, life-changing moment. Who was that woman?

52. "BBC" was the name for a famous Real Madrid trio--Karim Benzema, Gareth Bale and Cristiano Ronaldo.

Who are called "CMK" and also, the Bermuda Triangle, because the ball disappears for opposing teams when it reaches the three players?

53. Shakhtar Donetsk played Metalist 1925 of Kharkiv on August 23, 2022. It was a goalless draw. Why was the match so important?

54. Pele, English defender Bobby Moore and Argentinian midfielder Oswaldo Ardilles acted in *Escape to Victory*, a John Huston directed Hollywood film about Allied prisoners of war taking on a Nazi football team during the Second World War. The goalkeeper for the POW team was a top Hollywood star, who has acted as a boxer in several successful films. Name that Hollywood star.

55. It was this great German footballer's last game and in Kolkata. He was made honorary life member of Mohun Bagan and was gifted a trophy—a replica of a football studded with 8,640 diamonds. Name the footballer.

56. Giorgio Chiellini, captain of Italy and also Juventus, was one of the world's leading defenders. He has spoken about his toughest opponent. He had said: "I first played against (him) when he was 18...and he was unbelievable. I can't imagine what he's like now or what he can do in the future." Who is he talking about?

❑

ROUND 8

57. Benjamin Aguero, born in 2009, has football in his blood. His father, Sergio Aguero, played with distinction for Manchester City and 101 times for Argentina as a striker, scoring 41 goals. His mother is Giannina Maradona, daughter of Diego Maradona, one of the greatest footballers of all time. Benjamin Aguero also has a famous godfather, also a great sportsman. Who is that sportsman?

58. Jose Ramon Auto, a midfielder, was the first "foreigner," or someone not Spanish, to captain Real Madrid between 1942 and 1944. The second and third "foreigners" have been top-class players and they have won the captain's armband more recently. Identify them.

59. What do the following England players have in common: Gary Stevens, Peter Reid, Terry Butcher, Terry Fenwick and Peter Shilton?

60. Mohun Bagan and East Bengal have been playing since 1925, but the first hat-trick happened only on July 13, 1997, at the Salt Lake Stadium in Kolkata. Who scored the hat-trick?

61. Hope United, an initiative that has brought together men and women footballers is led by Gareth Southgate, England's manager. What does Hope United do? What does it fight?

62. Maria Rebello played for India. She also captained India's women's football team. She is the first, and therefore, an important name in the history of Indian football. What has she done in the international circuit?

63. The gold Predator Absolute is associated with French superstar Zinedine Zidane. What is the Predator Absolute?

64. He was the captain of the bronze medal-winning Indian team at the Asian Games in Bangkok in 1970. Later, a successful coach, he was the first to win the Arjuna and the Dronacharya awards. Name the person.

❑

ROUND 9

65. This is what Jurgen Klopp, the manager of Liverpool Football Club, said in 2021. "Who is better at this moment than him? That's clear. We don't have to talk about what Ronaldo and Messi did for world football and how they were really dominant, but in this moment, it is clear that there is no one better than him." Who is Klopp talking about?

66. The Ruhr Derby or the Revierderby, generally speaking, could mean a meeting between two clubs from the heavily industrialized Ruhr area, but more specifically, it is about the rivalry between two top clubs that have met hundreds of times since 1925. Which two clubs are we talking about?

67. On December 6, 2020, an Indian playing for Rangers FC, scored a goal. It was the first by an Indian in any game in European club football. The goal-scorer was a woman. Name the woman.

68. Cesar Menotti, coach of the 1978 World Cup-winning Argentina national team, was briefly part of Santos, Pele's club, in the late 1960s. He has said: "If Pele had not been born (he) would have been Pele." He was referring to one of Pele's Brazilian teammates. Who was the teammate?

69. On the morning of the 2002 World Cup final, FIFA organized a special football match between the two lowest-ranked football-playing countries in the world. So, on one hand, the two best countries—Brazil and Germany—and on the other hand, the two least successful countries. One of them was Montserrat. Name the other, an Asian country.

70. A German footballer, who played a major role in the 2014 World Cup victory, has spoken about the growing multiculturalism in his country's sporting ethos. He said: "My technique and my feeling for the ball is the Turkish side of my game and the always-give-your-all-attitude is the German side." He played 92 times for Germany. Name that footballer.

71. Petr Cech is one of the greatest goalkeepers of modern times, having played 333 times for Chelsea, 110 times for Arsenal, and 124 times for the Czech Republic. Cech has another passion: he plays for the Guildford Phoenix, a team based in Surrey, England. What does the Guildford Phoenix, a semi-professional team, play?

72. Vijay Barse founded the NGO Slum Soccer, to help underprivileged children. *Jhund*, a 2022 Bollywood film about Barse, written and directed by Nagraj Manjule, had a top star in the lead role. What is the name of the top star?

❑

ROUND 10

LIONEL MESSI

73. In 2005, long before Lionel Messi was acknowledged as one of the two greatest players of his generation, one player, one of the best of the time, predicted what was to come. "Watch this player. He will outdo us all." Messi admired him and once said he had the "ability to control the ball that makes me jealous." Who is the player, Messi's colleague for a while?

74. This is Lionel Messi talking about another footballer. "At first, it was weird after so many years of being rivals, being the two captains of Barcelona and Madrid, after so many Clasicos played, so many fights we had on the pitch. all that is in the past and we have always respected each other a lot, no matter how much we have been rivals in those Clasicos. Having him as a teammate today is spcctacular." Who is Messi referring to?

75. After receiving the Ballon d'Or for the seventh time in 2021, Messi (winner in 2009-12, 2015, and 2019) said: "Last year, everyone was in agreement to say you were the big winner of this award. Hopefully, France Football will give you the 2020 Ballon d'Or". The 2020 Ballon d'Or wasn't awarded because of the Covid outbreak. Who, according to Messi, deserved it in 2020?

76. When Messi moved from Barcelona to Paris Saint Germain, he said he was coming to a new country and had to start from scratch but "knowing that I had friends in the dressing room made me think that things would be easier to adapt to." His friends included Neymar and also, three Argentines: the coach and two players. Name them.

77. In 2022, Messi scored five goals for Argentina against Estonia. This isn't the first time that Messi has scored five goals in a match. He did that earlier in a club game. Who was Messi playing for? Who faced Messi at his best?

78. In 2010, this midfielder, an all time great, spoke about writing a novel on the 2014 World Cup in Brazil. In his novel, Brazil and Argentina would reach the final. Argentina would win 2-0 and Lionel Messi would score both goals. Name the footballer.

ROUND 10

79. Growing up, Messi almost always wore track suits. He read part of a biography of a famous player, but apparently didn't finish it. Name the player.

80. This is what Messi once said: "How lucky Andres is that he gets to score those goals, at the most crucial moments." Who is Messi referring to? And which crucial moment?

❑

ROUND 11

CRISTIANO RONALDO

81. Cristiano Ronaldo was the first player in men's football to score ten hat-tricks for his country. It happened in October 2021. Against which country?

82. Ronaldo's 100th Premier League goal was for Manchester United against Arsenal in April 2022. To whom did he dedicate his goal?

83. Ronaldo was born on February 5, 1985. In January 2021, days before he turned 37, he said: "Genetically,

I feel like I am... I am not going to say 25 because I'll be exaggerating, but around..." How old did Cristiano Ronaldo feel he was?

84. This is Ronaldo on Twitter. He said: "Sometimes, the result is not the one we fight for. Sometimes, the score is not the one we want. And this is on us, only on us, because there is no one else to blame. Our fans were, once again, amazing in their constant support. They deserve better than this, much better, and it is up to us to deliver. The time is now." The tweet came after a heavy defeat. To whom and by how much?

85. During the European championships in 2021, Ronaldo removed two bottles from the table during a press conference and the share price of the firm manufacturing the drink dropped by 1.6 percent or $US 4 billion. What had Ronaldo removed from the table?

86. When Ronaldo broke Josef Bican's record of 805 goals for club and country, he had scored 450 of the 807 goals for which institution?

87. Ronaldo posed naked for a magazine in June 2014 along with Irina Shayk, his girlfriend at that time. Which magazine?

88. Ronaldo is one of the first footballers with a private chef. He eats six small meals a day. He eats a lot of fish, particularly swordfish and tuna. His favourite dish is bacalhau a bras, which comprises potatoes, eggs, olives, onions and a certain kind of fish. Name that certain kind of fish?

❑

ROUND 12

89. A memorable statement about football was once made by one of the world's most infamous men. He said: "Abu-al Hasan told me a year ago. 'I saw in a dream, we were playing a soccer game against the Americans. When our team showed up in the field, they were all pilots!' He said: 'So, I wondered if that were a soccer game or a pilot game? Our players were pilots.' He said the game went on and we defeated them. That was a good omen for us." Who's speaking? In what context?

90. During every football game of this club, a part of the crowd begins chanting for independence 17 minutes and 14 seconds into the game. Which club? And why?

91. When he moved from Hyderabad in April 2021, ATK Mohun Bagan paid about ₹ 1 crore. At that time, it was the highest transfer fee in Indian football. He played for India and he's one of the best strikers. Name him.

ROUND 12

92. He played over a hundred times in the Indian Super League and a handful of times for India. This is what Sunil Chettri, his captain, has said about his hardworking ways. “He always calls me and says ‘Come, let’s do some crossing.’ Right foot. Left foot. Most of the time in training he does not get it right, but in matches he is precise.” Who is Sunil Chettri referring to?

93. His father died when he was seven and hadn’t gotten proper treatment as there weren’t any hospitals anywhere near his village. He ran away from home at 15 to become a footballer and 20 years later, in June 2021, he donated nearly $700,000 to build a hospital close to where he lived as a little boy. In 2019, he donated $350,000 to build a school. Who is the footballer?

94. Who is called “Pele in skirts”? She is still playing for Brazil and has scored over 110 goals while Pele scored 77 for the national team.

95. When Florentino Perez took over as President of Real Madrid, he wanted to recruit superstars. They have been called galacticos. The first recruit, from Barcelona in 2000, cost 62 million euros, more than it cost to get Ronaldo (42 million euros) or David Beckham (37 million euros) from Manchester United in 2003. Name the player.

96. Which national football team, since 2013, is called the Blue Tigers?

❑

ROUND 13

97. Didier Drogba, one of the greatest African footballers, played 254 times for Chelsea, scoring 104 goals and of course, 105 times for Ivory Coast, finding the net 65 times. He is such a cult figure that Drogbacite is an art form. What is Drogbacite?

98. Both Ronaldo and Ronaldinho, two of the greatest Brazilian players, considered this defender to be their toughest opponent. "It's impossible not to be amazed by how he made it all look effortless, especially when you got to play with him," Ronaldinho once said. Ronaldo said he was the "toughest ever" defender he'd faced. Who is he referring to?

99. Hugo Lloris has played 130 times for France and over 400 times for Tottenham Hotspur. As a youngster, he wanted to be a tennis player and was inspired by an all-time great player's serve-and-volley game. He has spoken about how similar, in some ways, the work of a goalkeeper and a tennis player is. Who is he a "big fan" of?

100. President Paul Kagame of Rwanda is a diehard supporter of an English Premicr League Club and frequently tweets about its performances. Additionally, a large number of African leaders like this club, whether it is William Ruto of Kenya, Atiku Abubakar of Nigeria, Rupiah Banda of Zambia, and many others. Name the club.

101. John Abraham acts as Sunny Bhasin in a football film set in England. Bhasin initially rejects Southall Football Club and joins Aston. Unhappy there, he rejoins Southall but accepts a lucrative contract from Gatwick and leaves. He changes his mind, returns, and helps Southall to win a critical match against Aston. Name the film.

102. When India played in the Olympics in 1948 in London, 1952 in Helsinki and 1956 in Melbourne, the football team captains belonged to one club. It is said that the selection of the captain was done keeping in mind the nationalistic appeal of the club. T. Ao led the national team in 1948, Sailen Manna in 1952, and 'Badru' Banerjee in 1956. Which club did they play for?

103. In March 2020, Neymar was on Instagram, photographed meditating, with a message: "Paris is our city, not yours." This was a message, a reply. To whom?

104. In 1989, for the first time, the Super Ballon d'Or was awarded. At that time, only Europeans were awarded the Ballon d'Or. Who was that person?

❑

ROUND 14

105. Sergio Ramos, who played 469 times for Real Madrid and 180 times for Spain, including as captain, is one of the most "carded" players in football history. He has 171 La Liga yellow cards and 20 red cards, the highest in the tournament's history. He has 24 yellow cards playing for Spain. How many red cards?

106. The International Federation of Football History and Statistics (IFFHS) has been awarded the World's Best Goalkeeper prize since 1987. It decided, in 1999, to award a World's Best Keeper of the 20th Century prize. He won, comfortably enough with 1,002 points and the runner-up getting 717. Who won?

107. A world-class player who represented his country 89 times, bought FC Bleid, a lower-division club in Belgium, and renamed it BX Brussels to run it as a social project for talented young people with few opportunities. Name the player.

ROUND 14

108. A brilliant striker, a World Cup winner, but also widely described as a bad boy, Romario played 70 times for Brazil scoring 55 goals, but after a challenging moment in his life, he joined politics and has been a Senator. He even ran for Governor of Rio de Janeiro. What was the challenging moment?

109. What, according to Carlo Ancelotti, who has coached Juventus, Chelsea, Paris Saint Germain, Bayern Munich and Real Madrid, "is the most important of the less important things in the world?"

110. Carlo Ancelotti, idolizes the lead character in one of the greatest Hollywood movies of all time. Speaking of the character, he asks in his autobiography: "Do you see a weak, quiet man or do you see a calm, powerful man in charge of the situation?"

111. The Tata Football Academy (TFA) was set up in 1987 and top Indian footballers including Chuni Goswami and Arun Ghosh served as directors. In 2017, TFA tied up with a top European club to improve facilities. Name the club. Many eminent footballers have played for the club, including French striker Antoine Griezmann and Spanish winger Carlos Aguilera.

112. Who was the first Brazilian sportsman, and of course, footballer, to be on the cover of Time magazine?

❑

ROUND 15

113. The Ballon d'Or was first awarded in 1956 and till 1995, it was given only to European footballers. After 1995, footballers playing in Europe were also considered, and only in 2007 were footballers from all over the world eligible. So, Pele has never won the Ballon d'Or though he was later awarded the Footballer of the century title. Till 2022, only four Brazilians have been awarded the Ballon d'Or. Ronaldo has won it twice. Who are the other three?

114. He was the first professional footballer to be a member of the Lok Sabha, being elected in 2013—it was a by-poll. He was re-elected in 2014. He played for India between 1974 and 1985, mostly in the midfield. Name him.

115. Great strikers can make a difference in a team's fortunes, whether it is a club or a country. In the 1986-87 Serie A season, AC Milan scored 31 goals.

The following year, AC Milan had a new striker, who, despite being injured for long periods, had scored 43 goals. The following year, when the striker was fully fit, AC Milan scored 61 goals. Who's the striker?

116. The same happened when another great striker joined Real Madrid. In 2001-02, Real Madrid managed 69 goals. The year after, Real Madrid scored 86 goals. Name the striker.

117. The International Federation of Football History and Statistics (IFFHS) has been awarding the World's Best Goalkeeper Award since 1987. Who is the first goalkeeper to win the award five times in a row? He won the award from 2008 to 2012.

118. Neymar's transfer fee from Barcelona to Paris Saint-Germain of 198 million Pounds Sterling in 2017 is a shattering figure. But at the turn of the century, in 1999, transfer figures were more modest. The record for 1999 was only 32 Million Pounds Sterling when this forward moved from Lazio to Inter Milan, where he stayed till 2005, playing 143 matches and scoring 101 goals. Who was the player?

119. Neymar, in 2014, was on the cover of Vogue Brazil magazine, along with a top fashion model. They were called Brazil's "dream team." Who was the fashion model?

120. A Brazilian striker died in Bangalore in 2004 after a collision with Mohun Bagan goalkeeper Subrata Paul during the Federation Cup final. Name the striker.

❑

ROUND 16

121. Ginza Tanaka, a Japanese jeweller, created a 25-kilogram solid gold replica of this footballer's left foot, priced at about $US 5 million. This was part of the effort to raise money for people hit by the earthquake and tsunami in 2011. Name the footballer.

122. In November 2000, FIFA announced that two players would jointly get the Player of the Century award. One had won the internet poll for all, getting 53 percent of the vote. The other had won the FIFA magazine readers and experts poll, getting 72 percent of the vote. Name the two footballers. Who had won what?

123. He was part of the Brazilian World Cup-winning side and a teammate of Pele's. After looking at Pele's list of the 125 greatest living footballers during the FIFA centenary, he was surprised and also angry that he wasn't one of the 125. Tearing up a piece of paper during a television programme, he said: "I respect his opinion, but I don't agree." There were a number of French footballers on the list, but apart from Zinedine Zidane, Just Fontaine, and Michel Platini, he couldn't believe he was "behind" the others. "This is a joke to have to hear this," he said. Who is the footballer?

124. As a coach, Jose Mourinho (Chelsea, Real Madrid, Manchester United, Inter Milan, and Roma), always called a spade a spade. Once, while coaching Real Madrid, he told a great player: "You're playing like Zidane and he's 50 years old!" The great player thought it funny, but effective and did well. Identify the player.

125. After Christian Eriksen collapsed while playing for Denmark against Finland, one of his friends dedicated to him the two goals he scored the next day. His message: "Chris. Strength, boy. Love you." Name him.

126. Before the Germany-Brazil semi-finals in the 2014 World Cup, Brazilian players David Luiz and Julio Cesar didn't stand to attention. They held up a shirt. Why?

127. Albacete Balompie is a third-tier Spanish football club though it has reached the La Liga level in the past. In 2011 and then, in 2013, it faced serious financial difficulties. A local boy, also a famous footballer, bailed the club out with a grant of 660,000 euros. Name the footballer, who played for Albacete as a young man, and then, 131 times for Spain.

128. All through the 1970s, Subhas Bhowmick was a high profile striker, either for Mohun Bagan or for East Bengal. Later, he would become a successful coach. At that time, he idolized a successful international coach and wrote to him asking for tips.

There was no reply. Bhowmick got hold of the coach's mobile number and called. Again, there was no response. Who's the famous coach?

❑

ROUND 17

129. Adel Abdessemed is a famous sculptor. One of his most famous sculptures is a 16 feet statue in bronze of an unfortunate event in a high-profile World Cup football match. It was unveiled at the Pompidou Centre in Paris on September 26, 2012. What had he depicted?

130. In the World Cup matches from 1930 to 2018, this team scored the maximum number of goals, more than any country: 229. Which country?

131. Who is Hope Solo? Why is Hope Solo a famous name in the world of football?

132. The women's team of West Ham, an English Premier League club, signed on an Indian in 2015. She played seven times for West Ham and now plays for Gokulam Kerala and the Indian team. She faced pressures at home. Her mother worried about her and her father, who served in the CRPF, grew enthusiastic about her career only after he saw her India jersey. Who is the player?

133. At the premiere of the Spanish film *Real, La Pelicula* or *Real, the Movie*, in 2005, Paul de Rio Canales, a Venezuelan painter, sculptor and revolutionary and Alfred di Stefano, the football great, were present. Why were they invited?

134. He was young, handsome and talented. After he scored twice in a club match against Benfica, the Portuguese press named him "El Beatle." Name the player?

135. Who, Footballer of the Year in 1993, is called Divine Ponytail as he is a devout Buddhist?

136. After Mohun Bagan won the IFA Shield, defeating East York in 1911, Sailen Bose, the club's secretary, had 12 special badges made, with a Royal Bengal tiger on them. The 11 players received their badges but Bose kept the 12th badge aside for someone who would be worthy of the heritage of the club. Who did Bose gift the 12th badge to several years later?

❑

ROUND 18

137. He was a centre-forward, short and overweight. When the President of Bayern Munich suggested his name, the coach said: "I don't want this elephant among my thoroughbreds" but did take him. He would prove his worth, not just to Bayern Munich, but also, the national team. Who was that player?

138. Ferenc Puskas, the Hungarian "Galloping Major" was one of the greatest strikers of all time. He was part of the all-conquering Hungarian side that reached the 1954 World Cup final and lost 2-3 to Germany. He played 84 times for Hungary, scoring 83 goals. But he also played four matches for another country. Name the country.

139. Alfred di Stefano was European Footballer of the Year in 1957 and 1959. One of the greatest footballers ever, he played for Real Madrid for over a decade and for three countries. Name those three countries.

140. He's short like Diego Maradona and has exceptional dribbling skills. Known as the Mampad Maradona, this Santosh Trophy star is a gifted striker. Name him.

141. My father was a national judo champion. My mother and sister were volleyball players, the latter having played for the national Under-21 side. My wife is a karate champion. I am a highly acclaimed football player. Who am I?

142. *United Passions*, released in 2014, was a football film starring Tim Roth, Sam Neill and Gerard Depardieu. Which controversial football personality was Roth acting as?

143. In 2017, this all-time great decided to play competitive tennis and he and his partner, Stefano Landonio, a 46-year old and once ranked 975, played in an ATP Challenger event, the Aspria Tennis Cup, in Milan. They offered little resistance and their opponents, Tomasz Bednarek of Poland and David Pel of Holland won 6-1, 6-1. After the match, the all time great said playing tennis was like "writing a poem after studying years of math." What was his name?

144. He was captain of the West Bengal cricket team, taking it to the Ranji Trophy finals. And he was captain of the Indian football team that won the gold medal in the 1962 Asian Games. Name the player.

❑

ROUND 19

145. Alfons Godall, Vice President of the Barca Foundation and a supporter of Catalan independence, resigned after a tweet, where he called a sportsman, an all-time great, a representative of the "enemy state." The sportsman, Alonso said, "has made me anxious from day one. I have it in the same bag as the red one (the Spanish football team, RM (Real Madrid), Alonso (racing-car driver Fernando Alonso) and everything that represents the enemy state." Name the sportsman, also a Real Madrid fan.

146. Rudolf Nureyev, the great dancer, told him he should have been a dancer. Jacques Tati, the French mine artist, said: "You are an artist. Your way of playing greatly resembles mine. We are two people who try to react instantaneously to situations that we haven't initiated ourselves." Name the great footballer.

147. Godfried Donkor, the famous artist from Ghana, has celebrated a great African footballer of the 60s and 70s in one of his paintings. The footballer never played for any African nation, but he's in the painting, as a saint with a halo. Who is the footballer?

148. The first Indian club to play in the Asian Football Confederation Champions League was FC Goa. Who was the first footballer to score for an Indian club in an AFC Champions League? This was against the powerful Persepolis of Iran.

149. Field Marshal Sam Manekshaw, after seeing him play, encouraged him to join the Indian Army. He was part of the bronze-medal team that participated in the 1970 Asian Games and one of India's most spectacular forwards, known for his bicycle kick. Who was that player?

150. When he was growing up, he was called Haginho, after the great Romanian midfielder of the 1990s by his friends. Today, he's one of the most accomplished footballers and his teammates call him "Il Professore" and "Radio" because of the way he directs his teammates, constantly talking with them during matches. Who?

151. One of the greatest footballers in recent years, he has scored over 550 goals for club and country. Prone to violence as an adolescent, he also liked stealing cars and motor-bikes. Once, he stole a postman's motor-bike and remembers it as a "great bike, a military bike." He also stole his football manager's bike, but was forgiven. Name the footballer.

152. Between 2008 and 2021, 13 Ballon d'Ors were awarded. There was no award in 2020. Of the 13,

ROUND 19

Lionel Messi has won seven, Cristiano Ronaldo has won five. Only one other footballer has won the award in this period. Who was that other footballer?

❑

ROUND 20

153. Eden Hazard, who captained Belgium and played over a hundred matches for his country, joined Real Madrid from Chelsea in 2019. He wanted the No. 10 jersey but Luca Modric refused and that year he wore a No. 50 jersey as a tribute to the 50th anniversary of a huge scientific achievement. What happened in 1969 that inspired Hazard?

154. Name the first side in the history of the English Premier League to receive 100 red cards. This happened during the 2020-21 season.

155. This was another "Hand of God" goal and that too against Napoli, a club Diego Maradona once played for. During a Napoli-Lazio match in September 2012, the referee awarded a goal to Lazio but took it back after the scorer, a German forward, informed the referee that he had handled the ball. The referee took back his decision and shook the forward's hand. The

Lazio forward has a reputation for fair play, besides being a prolific scorer. Name the player.

156. A very successful Nike advertisement featured a world-class defender with the slogan: "Italy's goalkeeper: easiest job in the world." Name the defender.

157. From 1992, the All India Football Federation or AIFF have been awarding Footballer of the Year prizes. The first winner was I.M. Vijayan. Who was the first person to be Footballer of the Year a record six times?

158. It was once called Studio São Paulo or São Paulo Stadium. It is now called Studio Diego Armando Maradona. Where is it?

159. In the 1960s, Pele was the top goal scorer of the decade, for club and country. He scored 403. Who were the top goal scorers in the 1970s and 1980s?

160. And who scored the most goals for club and country in the 90s and between 2000 and 2010?

❑

ROUND 21

JOHAN CRUYFF

161. Johan Cruyff, as a player and coach loved “beautiful football” and has been critical of winning ugly. After which World Cup match, an epic, Cruyff declared that the “beautiful” team lost to a “destructive” team. “It was a huge disappointment for the whole of football because after the World Cup teams started to play like” the ugly team did. Which two teams is Cruyff talking about? And which match?

ROUND 21

162. Johan Cruyff has spoken about two players he had coached and called them the most reasonable and far-sighted as any he had coached. "You could ask them for advice, because they could think about other people's problems," he has said. Who are the two players?

163. It has been called the Cruyff vs Cruyff World Cup final. Which World Cup final and why?

164. Once, Johan Cruyff, at a public reception in Holland, walked up to Queen Juliana to discuss something that was football related. "You're the Queen and maybe you can arrange something for us," he requested her. "Mr Cruyff," the Queen said, "you should speak to my minister of finance."What had Cruyff wanted?

165. Simon Kuper, author of *Soccernomics* and *Barca: the Rise and Fall of the World's Greatest Football Club*, speaks about the Cruyffian way—winning with beauty. Three teams, he has said, are doing that: a national team and two club teams. Which ones?

166. This is Johan Cruyff speaking about a great Brazilian player. "(He) could do what he wanted with the ball thanks to his enormous skill and vision. He knew where to position himself on the field of play. (He) wasn't quick, he didn't cross much and he wasn't a great header of the ball, but he made up for it with lots of other qualities. He was one of those players who did a little bit of everything, in the best sense of the word. (He) scored a lot of goals. In that sense he reminded me of Di Stefano." Who was Cruyff referring to?

167. When Johan Cruyff was being sacked, he told the official: "Why are you trying to shake my hand Judas?"

He added: "God will punish you for this deed." Which club was sacking Cruyff?

168. Being a top footballer, said Johan Cruyff, was like being a certain, very famous woman. People would look at her and think: "Loads of money, big house, I'd like to swap with her." But people never realised that she could never be herself or say what she thought." Who was Cruyff referring to?

❑

ROUND 22

169. Gerard Pique Bernabeu was part of Spain's 2010 World Cup winning side. He has played as centre-back for Spain over a hundred times and about 400 times for Barcelona. Pique is associated with a famous singer, with whom he has had two children. Name the singer.

170. Jurgen Klopp, coaching Borussia Dortmund in 2014, wanted to hire this great footballer. According to the footballer, Klopp wasn't impressed with the way he was wearing his baseball cap. Klopp thought he was like a rapper. Several years later, Klopp hired him. Name that footballer.

171. Zlatan Ibrahimovic is one of the most successful strikers in recent years with 550 goals for club and country. The Swedish Language Council has registered the verb "to Zlatan." What does it mean?

172. Zlatan Ibrahimovic again. His story is a rags to riches one. He grew up in a depressed working-class neighborhood, but in his mansion in Malmo, Sweden, there are no photographs of him, except one, that is of a body part. Which part of his body has Ibrahimovic photographed and put on display?

173. Xavier Hernandes Creus or "Xavi," a midfield general and now coach (505 games for Barcelona, 133 for Spain as a player) has spoken of a future after Cristiano Ronaldo and Lionel Messi retire. Four players, he has said, have the potential to be the best in the world. Neymar of Paris Saint Germain and Brazil is one of them. Who are the other three?

174. Raheem Sterling is an England regular. He has played regularly for Manchester City. He has said he doesn't like social media. "You're putting this information into your brain. You're going to feel down on yourself," he has said. What does he do, instead?

175. Paul Dybala, who plays for Juventus and Argentina as a striker, has an unusual way of celebrating when he scores a goal. He celebrates by covering his mouth with his hand, with his index finger pointing in one direction and his thumb in the other. It is the variation of a mask work by the lead actor in a Hollywood historical drama made in 2000. Name the film.

176. Eric Abidal, who played 67 times for France as a defender, was diagnosed with liver cancer in 2011. When he was battling cancer, his club teammate who's played over a hundred times for Brazil offered him part of his liver for a transplant. The operation was successful. Who's the Brazilian footballer?

❑

ROUND 23

177. When he was coach of San Lorenzo in the late 1990s, Alfio "Coco" Basile, who played and managed Argentina, didn't like a priest called Jorge Bergoglio blessing his players before the match; he felt the blessings were disturbing the players. So, he ensured the priest had no access to the dressing room. How is Jorge Bergoglio better known as?

178. In 2013, World Soccer magazine invited a galaxy of over 70 players, managers and experts from all over the world to choose the greatest team of all time, in 4-4-2 formation. The experts decided on Lev Yashin of the Soviet Union as goalkeeper and Paulo Maldini as one of the defenders. Who were the other three defenders?

179. Pele, inevitably, was one of the forwards, along with Lionel Messi in the lineup chosen by World Soccer's experts. Who were the four midfielders?

180. After playing 266 games for Liverpool, 80 for Manchester City and 26 for England (he scored seven times) he was fined and banned for four matches after an East Bengal-FC Goa match. Name the player.

181. Jorge Valdano was member of the Diego Maradona-led World Cup winning side of 1986. Which World Cup-winning side, for him was "the platonic dream of football?"

182. An all-time great, he wasn't very tall when he joined AC Milan. He was barely 1.64 metres tall or just above 5'4". The contract had a special clause saying he would get one million lire for every centimeters he grew beyond 1.70 metres or nearly 5'7". He would finally be 1.76 metres or 5'9". He never left the club, playing for it for 20 years, captaining it for 15. Name the player.

183. An all-time great Brazilian, he was sent off during a World Cup semi-final against Chile and only after the President of Brazil personally spoke with the authorities was he allowed to play. Brazil won, comprehensively, defeating Czechoslovakia 3-1 in the 1962 World Cup final. Who?

184. Graeme Souness, who captained Liverpool and played 54 times for Scotland, has said this about a contemporary player he calls a goal machine: "He is perhaps as greedy a player as I have seen. All the top names have an element of that but he is extremely selfish. Personal targets are important to him and he shoots from every possible angle, which frustrates his teammates at times. The other players accept it because he is so good." Name the player.

❑

ROUND 24

185. John Barnes, winger and then, midfielder, played 79 times for England in the 80s and 90s, scoring 11 goals. In his book, *The Uncomfortable Truth About Racism*, he has said that football cannot do anything about getting rid of racism. He has said the only way of destroying racism in society is by destroying what?

186. The government of Qatar owns which top European club through the state-run Qatar Sports Investments?

187. During the 2021 European Cup, the prices of shares of the firm manufacturing a product went down when Cristiano Ronaldo removed a bottle from the table before a press conference. When Paul Pogba removed a bottle, the stock price of the manufacturer actually went up by 1.7 per cent. What had Pogba removed from the table during the press briefing?

188. Pep Guardiola, one of the super coaches today, said this about which international player: "If I were reincarnated as a player, I want to be like him." It's a man who's played over 400 matches for Barcelona and over a hundred for Spain. Who is he referring to?

189. Michael Holding, the great West Indian cricketer, has spoken about his conversation with a prominent footballer. Before he was known in England, he went to a store in a hoodie and was followed all around the store. Then, he plays for Arsenal, scores a hat-trick and goes to the same store and its "Sir, what can I do for you?" Who is the player?

190. After letting in two goals in a crucial World Cup match, Brazilian goalkeeper Moacir Barbosa regarded the next 50 years of his life as a prison sentence. He was banned from visiting Brazilian teams during practice sessions because he would bring bad luck. When the goalposts he stood between during that match were sent to his house, he set them on fire. Which crucial World Cup match?

191. Zvonimar Boban of Croatia kicked a policeman beating up a Dinamo Zagreb supporter and became a nationalist icon.He became Chief of Football at the Union of European Football Associations, but during his tenure at FIFA in 2016, he helped to pioneer something revolutionary. What was that?

192. Which international footballer, also very successful in the English Premier League, called for a national campaign against child hunger during the COVID crisis? "I know what it feels to be hungry," he said during which he called for meals for children during the summer vacations.

❑

ROUND 25

193. A famous English player once said to Ronaldo, one of the recent Brazilian greats. "I remember you turning around to me and saying that the Brazil squad believed if there was any English player that could play in the Brazilian team it was me." Who is the English player?

194. When this great player was sold by Leeds to Manchester United for only 1 million Pound Sterling—an absolute steal—Brian Kidd, manager Alex Ferguson's assistant, was astonished. "Has he lost a leg or something?" he asked. He played for five years for Manchester United and 45 matches for France, scoring 20 goals. Name the footballer.

195. Vincente del Bosque Gonzalez played 445 times for Real Madrid and 18 times for Spain, mostly as a defensive midfielder. He was manager when Spain won the World Cup and of Real Madrid when it won the UEFA Champions League in 2000 and 2002. Yet, according to him one of the players was more important than he, the manager. Who was the player?

196. This was a must-win match. Playing against Brazil, the goalkeeper of this national side, Roberto Rojas, pretended he was injured, that a firecracker thrown by Brazilian fans had hit him. Actually, he had hidden a blade in his glove and deliberately cut himself. If he had been injured by a firecracker thrown by Brazilian fans, Brazil would have forfeited the match. The video footage showed what had happened and Rojas initially received a life ban and his teammates punished. The national team was banned from playing in the 1994 World Cup. Name the country.

197. What do the following players have in common: Mario Zagallo of Brazil, Franz Beckenbauer of West Germany and Didier Deschamps of France?

198. Andriy Shevchenko, who played over a hundred times for Ukraine was a child prodigy. But in 1986, when he was ten, his well-meaning mother set fire to his favourite football. Why?

199. Young men and women are eligible for the AIFF Emerging Player of the Year award. Since 2013, when the AIFF made the announcement, one male player has won the award twice, in 2017 and 2019-20. Name the player.

200. Karim Benzema of Real Madrid and France and also, Ballon d'Or winner, didn't quite approve of one of his colleagues, a brilliant young player, But now, they combine very well. "He's making much better choices. Before, he would beat a man and then, just go 'Let's see what happens.' Now, he'll know if he's going to shoot, cross or come inside. He's thinking things through." Who is Benzema talking about?

❑

ROUND 26

201. Playing for the Indian women's team in November 2021, Manisha Kalyan, receiving the ball from Priya Xaxa near the centre line, raced across and scored in the eighth minute of the game. It was the equalizer and the first time that India had scored a goal at the senior level, whether in the men's game or the women's, against this country. Which country?

202. More about Manisha Kalyan. Her instagram account was initially "mkd." The "m" and "k" are obvious enough, but the "d" is her nickname, which is the shortened version of a great Brazilian player's name. Name the Brazilian player?

203. He has played 142 times for his country and been part of a World Cup winning side. But his recent book—*White Thinking: Behind the Mask of Racial Identity*—is about racism. In the book, the author talks about a painting—Beating at Four Stakes in the Colonies—

by Marcel Verdier. It shows a White man whipping a Black slave, lying face down on the ground, as the slave-owner and his terrified young daughter watches. Name the player.

204. President Xi Jinping of China, a football fan, has spoken of his "three wishes" for Chinese football before 2050. The first wish is that the Chinese football team fights through the elimination rounds and takes part in the main event. What are the other two wishes?

205. Luca Modric, the Croatian captain, referred to a great footballer as "El Grande." Modric said: "When he took charge, he understood the demands of a great club like Real (Madrid). That's why he insisted we improve our physical condition. That's why training sessions under (him) became the most difficult since I had become a professional footballer." Who is Modric referring to?

206. Christian Vieri, once the world's highest paid footballer, has said he was very fond of another game, which he played regularly in school. In the Maldives on holiday in 2003, he regularly played with the cooks and waiters there. Which sport?

207. In 1997, the German captain led his team to the Yad Vashem Holocaust Memorial in Israel. The coach, former German player Berti Vogts, laid a wreath and the captain, one of Germany's leading strikers, said: "It is very, very emotional and also, shocking. Even if we are a younger generation, we still have the responsibility to talk and teach the next generation everything about what happened more than 50 years ago." Name the German captain.

208. He played 619 times for Roma, scoring 250 goals (and also 9 goals in 58 matches for Italy). Part of the 2006

ROUND 26

World Cup winning side he is called L'Ottavo Re di Roma or the Eighth King of Rome. Who?

❑

ROUND 27

209. At Old Trafford, Manchester United's home, is the famous United Trinity statue. It is a tribute to three great players, as the name "Trinity" suggests. Name them.

210. Till June 2020, the United States' soccer rules had stipulated that players have to stand during national anthems. That law changed in June 2020. Why?

211. The English Premier League is the richest football tournament in Europe with expected revenues of 6 billion Pound Sterling after a deal with NBC, the American TV network. Which are the next two richest tournaments?

212. Sandesh Jhingan, one of India's best defenders, is another player finding a place in European football. He has joined HNK Sibenik, a top-tier European club. In which country?

ROUND 27

213. No club has done as well in recent years in national leagues as Bayern Munich, winning uninterrupted between 2013 and 2022, a sign of incredible dominance. Which club won in 2012?

214. Football's next shining star could be a young man (born in 2000) and already an Olympic gold medalist. For the 2022-23 season, he was the most expensive transfer (from Ajax to Manchester United) at 95 million euro. Name the player.

215. Johan Cryuff, the great Dutch footballer, used to refer to certain players as "bread footballers." Who is a bread footballer?

216. In 2018, Baichang Bhutia, who has played 104 times for India, was asked to carry the Olympic torch. He refused, the first Indian sportsman to do so, as a gesture of support to suffering people in which part of the world?

❑

ROUND 28

PELE

217. It is an unusual moment. A statue of a great footballer, still alive, is being unveiled in Stoke City, a small English town. Among the chief guests is Pele and Nobel laureate in Peace, Archbishop Desmond Tutu. This was in 2008. Name the footballer, highly regarded by Pele.

218. Pele's last game was in October 1977. He played for both sides, one half for each club team. Name the two club teams.

ROUND 28

219. In his early days, he was called Dico by his family members and Gasolina by some of his team members. What did he prefer being called?

220. Tarcisio Burgnich, played 358 games for Inter Milan and 66 times for Italy, mostly as a defender. He was called "The Rock." He was given the responsibility of marking Pele, and it was an important match. He would say later: "I told myself before the game 'he's made of skin and bones just like everyone else,' but I was wrong." Name the important match.

221. Edinho, a goalkeeper, played 200 club games and has also been a coach and manager. How is he linked to Pele?

222. What, in 2022, did Pele refer to as "unjustifiable?" He said: "No argument exists that can justify violence."

223. Pele never played for a European club. He was dissuaded from going by Clive Toye, a British football administrator, who said: "Don't go to Italy. Don't get to Spain. All you can do is win a championship." Toye invited him to "win a country." Pele agreed. What happened?

224. Andy Warhol, the artist, spoke of 15 minutes of fame for everyone.With Pele, he broke his usual rule. It wasn't 15 minutes, it was much, much more. How much time for Pele?

❑

ROUND 29

DIEGO MARADONA

225. In Kolkata, after being shown an album of photographs, he said: "Castro is my friend and anyone who is Castro's friend is my friend." Who, as a result, became his friend?

226. Diego Maradona and Angel Cappa, who coached River Plate, one of Argentina's top football clubs, were watching a great sportsman in action. Replying to Cappa, Maradona said: "He's great. I admire him too, but never forget that the guy plays with his hands." Who was Maradona referring to?

227. A great player has spoken about a meeting with Diego Maradona, who was wearing two wristwatches. "I asked him why he was wearing two, and he said his daughter had given them to him as a present and since then, had never taken them off. At the end of the meal, he took one off and gave it to me as a gift." Maradona was so insistent that the great player was forced to accept the watch. Who was the player?

228. Maradona once said about an important moment in the history of football: "I was waiting for my teammates to embrace me, and no one came…I told them, 'Come hug me or the referee isn't going to allow it.' " What had happened?

229. In the same match against England, Maradona scored what has been called the "Goal of the Century," when he dribbled past five English players and scored. Maradona always maintained he wanted to pass the ball to one of his colleagues and only because he was "surrounded" and "had no space" that he had to continue the play and finish it. Who had he wanted to pass it to?

230. While the goal against England was the "Goal of the Century," another one by Maradona came fourth—the fourth best of the century. Which goal?

231. In the 1994 World Cup, after a 2-1 win over Nigeria, Maradona failed a drug test. What banned drug was found in his blood sample?

232. This is what one of Maradona's teammates and admirers once said: "If Jesus Christ rose again on the third day, which isn't easy, Maradona rose again at least three times, which isn't easy either." Who was the teammate?

❑

ROUND 30

233. Xavi Hernandez Creus, a gifted midfielder was part of the 2010 Spanish World Cup winning team. He was so keen on coaching Barcelona that he said "No" to a national side. Name the country.

234. The "El Clasico" in football is a match between Barcelona and Real Madrid. Which two German teams play in the Der Klassiker or the German Clasico?

235. The French too have something similar for the last 50 years, the two clubs having been head-to-head over a hundred times. Name the two clubs.

236. Mauricio Pochettino Troserro once played for Argentina (20 caps) and has been coaching top clubs for decades. He once spoke about a top player: "He's the best, one of the best in football history. What surprises you is the way he behaves. He waits for treatment; he goes to the canteen and waits in queue for the food. It is amazing to see him behave in this way because he is an amazing player behaving like a normal player." Who is he referring to?

237. A club match between National PR and Atletico Paranaense on May 3, 2015, was an important moment for India as an Indian footballer played in the match. He came on as a substitute in the 67th minute. It was the first time that an Indian had played at this level in Brazil. Who was the Indian player?

238. FC Goa, which began life in 2014, is one of India's top football clubs. Which leading Indian cricketer is co-owner of the club?

239. Dior, the French fashion house, appointed a top footballer as its global ambassador. The footballer, in a tweet, said he'll be collaborating with Dior in areas of men's fashion and cologne. Name the footballer.

240. One of the most iconic TV football advertisements was Nike's Airport '98, shot with Brazilian footballers in airports. This was Nike's campaign in the wake of Adidas being the official sponsors of the 1998 Football World Cup. This is what Nike's Pierre-Laurent Baudey said about one Brazilian footballer: "He had a ton of charisma. His scene was one the art director was worried about. So, when we asked him to kick it through the X-Ray machine, all of us were watching and he did it first time. We had to say: 'Hey, one more time,' because it was so incredible. Who was the footballer?

❑

ROUND 31

241. During meals, this great footballer starts with dessert and then, moves to the starter and the main course, on the advice of his wife Anna, a nutrition specialist. He sleeps on his left side after speaking with a sleep therapist to keep his stronger right leg in good shape. He's been known to read books on breathing and coach Pep Guardiola calls him "The most professional footballer I have ever met. He thinks about the right food, sleep and training 24 hours a day." Name the footballer.

242. Juan Camilo Zuniga, a defender who played 61 times for Colombia, caused serious damage to a Brazilian footballer and as a result, Brazil's football fortunes. What had he done?

243. Carlo Ancelotti, the famous coach, has spoken about one of his greatest mistakes. As Parma coach, he had the opportunity to sign on a great footballer. But the footballer wanted to be a playmaker and Ancelotti wanted him to be a striker. Eventually, the footballer went to another club and was wildly successful. He scored 25 (actually 22 goals) for Bologna and I lost 25 goals. Big mistake." Who is the player?

244. The Best FIFA Men's Player Award for 2021 went to Robert Lewandowski, narrowly edging out Lionel Messi. He, as the Polish captain, could vote. He voted for Messi as the second-best player and Cristiano Ronaldo as the third-best player. Who did he vote for as Best Player?

245. This leading footballer is also a UNICEF ambassador. He has dreamt of a world "where children grow up safe—safe from violence, war, poverty, hunger and preventable disease. A world in which all children have the opportunity to reach their full potential. Together, we need to imagine a better future for every child and make sure that we achieve it." Who is the footballer?

246. Michel Platini, French captain and midfield general in the 80s, won the Ballon d'Or three times in a row, once said that what Zinedine Zidane could do with a ball, Diego Maradona could do with what?

247. Michel Platini, who played 72 times for France, scoring 42 goals, came out of retirement in 1989 and played an international against the Soviet Union for a Gulf state. He played for about 20 minutes at the request of the ruler. The Soviet Union won 2-0.

248. The 'trequartista,' like the libero, is a relatively new position in football. Where does a trequartista station himself (or herself) and what is his (or her) role?

❑

ROUND 32

249. “Just as we were about to land and some of us looked down, all we could see was a sea of people. There were thousands of people at the airport, and one of the players, Girgio Chinalia, said to me: “How could we land here!’ There was anxiety in his voice.” This is Pele speaking. Where were they landing? What was happening?

250. “Welcome to the club.” was Pele’s tweet on July 15, 2018. Who was the tweet for? And why?

251. Telugu film stars Nagarjuna and Chiranjeevi own the Kerala Blasters Football Club, which participates in the Indian Super League. For a long while, a cricketing great had a 20 per cent stake in the club. “My heart will always beat for the Kerala Blasters,” he had said. Name the cricketer.

252. The West German team in the early 80s, Pele had jokingly said was one player “and ten robots,” a reference to the technical similarity of the players and also, their namelessness and facelessness. He did mention the one player, who played 95 times for West Germany, scoring 45 times, by name. Identify the player.

253. This great Brazilian player, speaking about racism in football, regretted how "Black people" suffer and mentioned that he was White. This led to much debate and his father, Nelio Nazario, said:" He knows very well that he is Black. His father is Black, and so, that does not make sense." Nazario felt his son was trying to make a philosophical point. Later, the player clarified. He said he was trying to say that his skin tone was lighter and therefore, hadn't faced any prejudice in Europe. Name the player.

254. One of the greatest practitioners of "beautiful football," Johan Cryuff had to say this. "This, ugly, hard, hermetic, hardly eye-catching football style. If with this they got satisfaction, fine, but they lost." He added that it hurt him that "such an ugly path to the final" was chosen. Which team is Cryuff talking about?

255. Part of his preparations for the European Cup 2011, was a long essay on patriotism, entitled "Dear England." This essay included references to the need for equality and to fight racial injustice. Who was the person?

256. Germany and Argentina faced each other in the final of the 1986 and 1990 World Cups. Both sides won once. During both occasions, Diego Maradona, the captain of Argentina, exchanged jerseys with a top German player. Name the player.

❑

ROUND 33

257. This is what Indian striker Jeje Lalpekhlua, who has played over 50 times for India and scored over 20 goals, has said about a famous Indian cricketer. "He may have been a goalkeeper back in school. But when he's playing, it has been evident that his skills with his feet have not left him. He's quite good at football, to be honest," he said. Which cricketer?

258. A very successful goalkeeper, he is one of the most tattooed players. Addicted to being tattooed, he has said, he has tattoos of an angel's wings on his chest and also, a dove, with the words "I belong to Jesus." On his knuckles are the words "Dues e fiel" or "God is faithful" and on his arm, some rosary beads. On his back, he has an eagle and a lion, and on his left arm, an owl. There's more, but who's the player?

259. His father played for Kenya. He's named after a famous Serbian basketball player who played for L.A. Lakers for many years. And he's a regular for Belgium and also, AC Milan. Name the footballer, who's also had a dolphin named after him.

260. *The Two Escobars* is a highly-rated, if tragic, documentary on football and crime, or more specifically, how the drug-trade influenced football. One Escobar is, of course, Pablo Escobar, the drug lord. Who is the other Escobar?

261. One of the most controversial players, he turned from villain to hero before retiring early after a series of injuries. He was involved in the Totonero match-fixing scandal and banned for two years, and on returning, guided Italy to the World Championships in 1982. He scored a goal in the 3-1 win over West Germany in the final and was awarded the Ballon d'Or. Who is the player?

262. During one of the most memorable World Cup games, this player was carried off after being assaulted by an opponent. Michel Platini, playing in the game, later said he thought his compatriot was dead. "He had no pulse. He looked so pale." Name the severely injured player. And the match.

263. In the same match, the referee did not reprimand the person responsible for the assault. The "attacker" expressed no remorse for the assault. When told that the player he had assaulted had lost two teeth, he reportedly said: "If all that's wrong, I will pay for the crowns." Who was the player?

264. He's one of the greatest Asian footballers of all time. He represented his country over a hundred times and has played regularly in Europe—for Bayer Leverkusen and Tottenham Hotspurs. He's also a brand ambassador for Burberry, the luxury fashion house, and is known to have dated pop singers. Name the footballer.

❑

ROUND 34

265. He was the first sportsman to have 10 million followers on Twitter. He has more now, both on Twitter and Facebook. He is also the United Nations World Food Programme's Ambassador against Hunger. Name the footballer.

266. Abedi Ayew, one of the greatest footballers of the generation, played 73 times for Ghana, scoring 19 goals. He spent years playing for Lille and Marseille. In the world of football, as a mark of respect for his ability, he has a special name. What is he called?

267. Levin Mete Oztunali has played junior German teams at various levels, being part of the winning European Under-19 and Under-21 championships. His grandfather was one of West Germany's great players, representing his country in four World Cup tournaments and scoring 43 times in 72 matches. Name him.

268. He is the oldest player to have won the World Cup, at 40! More importantly, as goalkeeper, he did not concede a goal in an international match for 1,142 minutes, a record that may never be broken. Name the player.

269. This great Australian cricketer initially wanted to be a football player and played, in 1988, for St Kilda's Football Club's under-19 team. He was promoted to the reserves team, but that's when he began to concentrate on cricket. Name the player.

270. Six months into a bitter war where hand-to-hand fighting has been the norm, soldiers on both sides decided that they'd had enough, laid down their weapons and famously, played football on Christmas Day. Some soldiers even wrote home about their experiences about a couple of days of peace when the guns fell silent and football matches, some of them improvised, happened. Which war?

271. Reverend William Pettigrew introduced football in this part of British-ruled India in 1899. Students of John Stone School, where he taught, played football. Over a hundred years later, the Santosh Trophy went to the state where Pettigrew taught. Which state?

272. Mohun Bagan won the IFA Shield in 1911 defeating East Yorkshire regiment 2-1. Which Indian club won the Durand Cup in Delhi defeating the Royal Warwickshire Regiment 2-1 in India? This win also helped the Indian freedom movement.

❑

ROUND 35

AFRICAN FOOTBALLERS

273. He is the only footballer to be awarded FIFA Footballer of the Year, winner of the Ballon d'Or and more importantly, the President of his country in 2018. Name the footballer.

274. He won the African Footballer of the Year four times, and the Olympic gold medal in 2000 and played with distinction for Barcelona and Inter Milan scoring 108 and 33 times for them respectively. Name the footballer.

275. Pierre-Emerick Emiliano Aubameyang joined AC Milan's Youth Academy, played for Saint-Atienne, Borussia Dortmund, Arsenal and is now with Chelsea. He's a Spanish citizen, but which country does he play for, having scored about 30 goals?

276. He is of African origin, but he plays for a European country. His mother tongue is Congolese Swahili, but he speaks French, German, Dutch, English, Flemish, Spanish, Portuguese and Italian. Who is the player?

277. Sol Bamba, a centre-back, began his career with Paris Saint Germain and has played for Leicester City, Palermo, Hibernian and Middlesborough. He has played over 40 times for which African country?

278. Junior Fashion Sakala is a rising star. He's a striker for Rangers, a Scottish club. He's played 19 times for his country. Which country?

279. Augustine Azuka Okacha was a member of three World Cup squads of his country. An attacking midfielder, he has played over 70 times for his national team, scoring over a dozen goals apart from four years at Paris Saint Germain. Which country does he represent?

280. Wilfried or Dazet Wilfried Armel Zaha has played over 250 times for Crystal Palace. He is a key striker. Which country does he play for, apart from the two games for England?

❑

ROUND 36

281. Gerard Piqué, who played 102 matches for Spain, has invested heavily in one of the oldest sporting events. He's keen on completely revamping this tournament. Name the tournament.

282. Erling Haaland could be the next great striker. He has already done wonders for Red Bull Salzburg in Austria, Borussia Dortmund in Germany and has begun well for Manchester City in England. He was born in Leeds, England, but which country does he play for?

283. Haaland again. He, along with Erik Botheim and Erik Tobias Sandberg, two of teammates from his days in the national U-18 squad, have formed Flow Kingz. What is it?

284. This is Roger Federer, one of the greatest tennis players of all time, talking about his favourite footballer. "What I love about (him) probably most is when he gets the ball and is able to turn the body towards goal, and then, he has full vision. Then he's going to pass, or dribble, or shoot. There's always three options for him. He's one of the few who's got that." Who is Federer referring to?

285. In his memoirs, Nobel laureate in Economics Amartya Sen speaks of the economic consequences of matches between Mohun Bagan and East Bengal. What happens?

286. Antoine Griezmann, the forward, and part of the 2018 World Cup-winning team, was rejected by several youth academies in France as a pre-teen and even later. What went against him?

287. Which England football captain was arrested for stealing an expensive bracelet from a jewellery store in Bogota, Colombia? He was subsequently cleared.

288. Weltvogel Park in Germany is one of the world's largest bird parks. It's ambassador is a leading footballer, also the author of an autobiography, *Keep it Simple*. Name the footballer.

❑

ROUND 37

289. This Nobel laureate in literature was also a football coach in the 1960s and devised the "4-4-1-0 absent forward" idea. He said a "match was simply a series of individual battles in which the opposition were attempting to deny players freedom simply by predicting their future actions based on what their past actions had been. That is why I preached the infinite choices that were available to the lads at all times keeping in mind the rules, of course." Name the Nobel laureate.

290. *Saaheb*, an 80s Bollywood film, is about Sunil, an aspiring footballer, but widely regarded by his family as a failure. His family in is financial trouble, so he decides to sell his kidney to raise funds for his sister's wedding and is therefore forced to give up football. Who is the Saheb in the film?

291. He began his career in 2006 for his country's Under-21 team. He was playing as a left-back in club football, beginning with Southampton. Soon after, he was playing for his country's senior team and he wasn't even 17. People noticed he was quick and moved him to the forward line. He has played over 100 times for his country. Name the player.

292. In January 2020, this Brazilian footballer with more than 50 caps, became a born-again Christian. Afterwards, he wrote on Instagram: "I gave you my failures and I will give you my victories too… My greatest title is your love, Jesus." Who is this Brazilian footballer?

293. He played 80 times for England, scoring 48 goals. He also played cricket as a teenager, captaining Leicestershire Schools. He is remembered as a potent striker. Name the player.

294. Angelo Ogbonna is an Italian and has played for Torino and Juventus and also, the Italian national team. He was born in Italy after his parents moved there from an African country with a good footballing record. Which country?

295. Kylian Mbappe, perhaps the greatest player of his generation, has said: "If you tell yourself that you'll do better than them, it's beyond ego or determination—it's lack of awareness. Those players are incomparable. They have broken all laws of statistics." Name the players he is talking about.

296. His father was a daily wage labourer and his mother, a maid. His father died when he was 12 and he barely had enough to eat. He would become one of India's all-time greats. George Blues, the FC Kochi coach, has said that if he had been born in Europe, given adequate nutrition and supplements, he would have become an international star. Who is he referring to?

❑

ROUND 38

297. What do the following have in common: Cristiano Ronaldo's CR7, Zlatan Ibrahimovic's A-Z, Rio Ferdinand's FIVE Supply and Kevin De Bruyne's KDB?

298. Award-winning director Ken Loach's film *Looking for Eric* is about Eric Bishop (Steve Evets), a postman. Very down and out, he is inspired by a great footballer, who appears in the film. Name the footballer.

299. The women's team of this country is named The Matildas. And the men's team is called The Socceroos. Which country, not immediately associated with football, but a rising power?

300. Liverpool was playing West Bromwich Albion in an English Premier League match on May 16, 2021. In the 96th minute, seconds before the final whistle, an unusual goal happened after Trent-Alexander Arnold's corner. It was a rare event. An unlikely person scored. Who was the person?

301. Mauricio Pochettino Trossero, who played 20 times for Argentina and is now a top coach, has said this about three players, in the same team. "All three players can be king of any club in the world. But you have three kings in the same club, three players who need different things from the team." Name the three players.

302. When Alex Sanchez scored the decisive penalty in the Copa America final against Argentina, he helped his country to win the Copa America for the first time in a century. Today, he is the face of his country's export campaign. Which country?

303. This country, somewhat unexpectedly, won the Women's World Cup in 2011. Before the quarter-final against Germany and the semi-final against Sweden, the team's coach showed the players footage of a catastrophe that had hit the country to build resolve. Which country? And what catastrophe?

304. One of the best foreign players to play in India in the 70s and 80s had come to study at the Aligarh Muslim University after playing in the 1978 World Cup. He played with great mastery for a decade. Name the player.

❑

ROUND 39

305. Pickles, a pet dog, saved the international football community from considerable embarrassment in 1966, just before the World Cup. How?

306. Found by Pickles, it disappeared again some years later. Where is it now?

307. Before his retirement game in 2023, a canvas laid on the ground near the centre circle said: "Sempr3. All his teammates had his name on the backs of their football jerseys. Sempr is Catalan for "always" and 3 was his jersey number. Name the player.

308. He was one of the greatest strikers. Paolo Maldini, the legendary defender, said about him: "Right foot. Left foot. Heading, so strong, fast. He could score. He could pass the ball. The way he played was timeless." He has been called the Swan of Utrecht. Name the striker.

309. Indian international and then coach, P.K. Banerjee, called this footballer who played in Kolkata "the king of kings." He played for East Bengal, Mohammedan Sporting and Mohun Bagan between 1966 and 1984, excelling year after year. He was affectionately called Bade Mian or the Big Gentleman. Name the footballer.

310. What do the following German players have in common: Thomas Muller, Miroslav Klose, Toni Kroos, Sami Khedira and Andre Schurrle? This relates to the events of a single match.

311. One of the greatest club games was between Real Madrid and Eintracht Frankfurt in May 1960. Real Madrid won 7-3 with Alfredo di Stefano scoring three times. A great player scored the other four goals, in a space of 27 minutes. Who was the great player?

312. Franz Beckenbauer, who won the World Cup as player and coach, was called "Kaiser." Which great defender, captain of his country, having led his team to a World Cup final, was called "Kaiser Franz"?

❑

ROUND 40

313. For several years, beginning 1988, three great Dutch players— Marco van Basten, Rudd Gullit and Frank Rijkaard— played a major role in AC Milan's success. The money to get them was found by the club president who became a major politician. Name the person.

314. In 2015, Diego Maradona visited Tunisia and met Ali Bin Nasser or Ali Bennaceur called him his "eternal friend" and presented with an Argentina jersey. Who is Nasser and why did Maradona thank him?

315. India won the Nehru Cup in 2007 and 2009 and also, the AFC Challenge Cup in 2008. Such success was unprecedented at that time. Who was the coach, a foreigner?

316. A new "position" was born in football in Switzerland between the two World Wars. A defender would stand behind the back line and move to the right or left to deal with attacks. It was called the "verrou" or bolt. In which country did this become the norm in the 1950s? It was called the catenaccio.

317. It wasn't about David and Goliath, it was about David defeating many Goliaths. One of the most underrated teams in the 2004 European Cup, this national team, coached by a German, defeated France in the quarter-final, the Czech Republic in the semi-final and the hosts, Portugal in the final. Even the team, without star players, wouldn't have imagined it. Which country?

318. It began life as Bicholim Football Club. It would be the first Goan club to win the Rovers Cup in Mumbai in 1974-75. The trailblazing coach was Joseph Rathnam. Name the club.

319. Diego Maradona had a tattoo of a man he called his second father on his leg. When he died, Maradona said: "I want to thank him for everything." Who was the person?

320. In Gowthampura, a suburb in Bangalore, there's a statue of a footballer, not from Bangalore or Karnataka or even, India. It may be a sign of what local footballers want to be. Bhaichung Bhutia and I.M. Vijayan were present when it was unveiled. Whose statue?

ANSWERS

ROUND 1

1. Pele, one of the greatest footballers of all time. He was part of Brazil's World Cup winning side in 1958, 1962 and 1970.

2. East Bengal Football Club.

3. Ernesto "Che" Guevara, the revolutionary who helped Fidel Castro to overthrow the regime the Cuba.

4. Ronaldo or Ronaldo Luis Nazario de Lima, one of the Brazil's greatest stars. He played an important role in Brazil's World Cup victory in 2002, scoring in the final.

5. Pep Guardiola, currently coaching Manchester City. A good player in his time, he has coached Barcelona and Bayern Munich.

6. A leg injury after being hit by a car.

7. Xi Jinping, the Chinese leader. He is General Secretary of the all-powerful Chinese Communist Party.

8. Sunil Chhetri, one of India's greatest strikers. He has scored more than 80 goals for India.

ROUND 2

9. The Naxalite agitation was still continuing in Kolkata and Ray felt that the presence of top players would encourage young men to watch the matches and not join the movement. A successful Calcutta League and the IFA Shield would lead to less violence.

10. Colombia. The difference between the two sides was an own goal.

11. Holland and Belgium.

12. Austria (he scored 14 goals in 19 matches) and Czechoslovakia (12 goals in 14 matches). He also played a match for Bohemia and Moravia.

13. Ajay Devgan, a national award winning actor. He has also directed and produced films.

14. China and India. Neither country, despite having populations of over 1 billion, is a football power today.

15. For people, primarily Ukranians, displaced by the war between Ukraine and Russia.

16. North Macedonia. Despite the victory, North Macedonia could not qualify for the World Cup tournament in Qatar after losing to Portugal.

ROUND 3

17. Alexia Putellas of Spain and also Barcelona, with 150 plus goals for club and country.

18. Garrincha or Manuel Francisco dos Santos, the great dribbler. He played 50 times for Brazil, scoring 12 goals.

19. Nelson Mandela. South Africa. This was in 1996. Three members of the national team, including the captain, Neil Tovey, were White.

20. Mahendra Singh Dhoni, who captained the Indian cricket team, and Abhishek Bachchan.

21. Roman Abramovich, the Russian businessman. He bought Chelsea Football Club soon after.

22. Parminder Nagra. She acted as Jess.

23. Borussia Dortmund, a German club founded in 1909.

24. Richarlison. A spectator had thrown a banana after Richarlison was celebrating scoring a goal, Brazil's second.

ROUND 4

25. Baichung Bhutia. He has also been a Trinamool Congress candidate in different elections, but was not very successful.

26. Manchester United, with 1,415.

27. A goalkeeper usually dives towards his left or right when a penalty kick is taken. A Panenka is a shot directed towards the centre of the goal, taking into account the goalkeeper has dived to his left or right. it is often taken gently, without much force.

28. Diego Maradona's jersey. This was the jersey Maradona wore in the match against England in 1986 when he scored the "hand of God" goal and also, one of the greatest goals ever, after dodging past five English players. Hodge and Maradona had exchanged jerseys after the match.

29. This was the first match between the women's teams of the two clubs.

30. Sajal Bag, a midfielder, who plays for Mohun Bagan.

31. Flamengo, in Rio de Janeiro. It's still called the Flamengo Rowing Club or the Clube de Regatas do Flamengo. The club's greatest son is Zico with 732 appearances and 509 goals.

32. Gareth Bale of Wales, one of the world's highest-paid footballers. He called the article "slanderous and derogatory." He played 176 times for Real Madrid, scoring 81 goals and over 100 times for Wales with 40 strikes to his credit.

ROUND 5

33. Southampton FC. He's been a Southampton supporter for years. It's his 'local' club.

34. The three women shortlisted to be referees for the men's World Cup Football Championships 2022.

35. Albert Camus in 1957. He is remembered for novels like *The Stranger* and *The Plague*.

36. Mohun Bagan's victory over the East Yorkshire Regiment team in 1911. Mohun Bagan, the first Indian team to do so, won 2-1, with Abhilash Ghosh scoring the match-winner.

37. Mexico, in 1986. Argentina, led by Diego Maradona, were the champions.

38. Neymar, the Brazilian captain and also, Paris Saint Germain star. As he himself said: "I was able to make my dream come true and be part of my favourite show."

39. Neville D'Souza, the centre forward. He scored three of the four goals in the victory over Australia.

40. Ian Botham. Captain of England for a while, he played 102 tests scoring 5,200 runs and taking 383 wickets. In 116 one day internationals, he scored 2,113 runs and took 145 wickets.

ROUND 6

41. East Bengal. Between 1949 and 1953, East Bengal scored 386 goals, an extraordinary number.

42. Ronaldinho. He celebrated his 40th birthday in jail.

43. Ghana. In between, Senegal reached the quarter-finals in 2002.

44. Bibin Ajayan. He joined the Golden Threads.

45. Qatar. It is in Doha's Sports City, close to the Khalifa International Stadium.

46. Thibaut Corutois, the Real Madrid (and Belgian) goalkeeper, who made some match-winning saves. He spoke out after Real Madrid defeated Liverpool 1-0 to win the Champions League in 2022.

47. Pep Guardiola, the Manchester City manager, and his Liverpool counterpart, Jurgen Klopp.

48. It is a one-off match between the best European nation, winner of the UEFA (Union of European Football Associations) Cup and the CONMEBOL or the South American Football Confederation's Copa America. In 2022, Argentina defeated Italy 3-0, with Lautaro Martinez, Angel di Maria and Paulo Dybala scoring. The man of the match was Lionel Messi.

ROUND 7

49. Barcelona, one of the top Spanish clubs.

50. Pradip Kumar or P.K. Banerjee, also a very successful coach.

51. Chloe Kelly, who scored the winning goal for England in the Women's Euro Cup final. She was talking about taking off her shirt right after scoring the goal.

52. Casemiro of Brazil, Luca Modric of Croatia and Toni Kroos of Germany. They played for Real Madrid, the name coming from the manager Carlo Ancelotti.

53. It was the first match of the Ukrainian Premier League after the war with Russia began.

54. Sylvester Stallone. His "Rocky" films were big hits.

55. Oliver Kahn, the German captain. Kahn, in his time, was one of the world's leading goalkeepers.

56. Kylian Mbappe of France and Paris Saint Germain.

ROUND 8

57. Lionel Messi, one of the greatest players in contemporary football.

58. Marcelo Viera, the Brazilian left back, who played 386 times for Real Madrid and 58 times for the Brazilian senior team. He was captain till 2022 before handing over to French forward and Ballon d'Or winner Karim Benzema.

59. These were the players (Reid was a defensive midfielder, Shilton, the goalkeeper and the others, defenders), Diego Maradona dribbled past to score the goal of the century in the 1986 World Cup. Argentina defeated England 2-1 (Maradona scored the "Hand of God" goal in this match) and went on to become world champions.

60. Baichung Bhutia. East Bengal won 4-1.

61. Misogyny. Southgate has said "men can do better."

62. Rebello is the first FIFA-listed woman referee from India. She is also the first woman referee in the I League.

63. This was the football boot Zinedine Zidane wore during the 2006 World Cup final against Italy. It was in this match that Zidane headbutted Italian player Marco Materazzi. Adidas reintroduced the boot before the 2022 World Cup.

64. Syed Nayeemuddin. The All India Football Federation sacked him after India lost 0-3 to Yemen in the 2006 World Cup qualifiers.

ROUND 9

65. Mohammed Salah, an Egyptian striker. He plays for Liverpool.

66. Borussia Dortmund and FC Schalke 04.

67. Ngangom Bala Devi, who has played for Manipur Police and over 50 times for India. Rangers defeated Motherwell Football Club 9-0, Devi scoring the final goal.

68. Tostao. He played 54 times for Brazil (1966-72) and scored 32 times. He played for Cruziero.

69. Bhutan. Bhutan won 4-0, the match being played in Thimpu. There's a documentary on the match, called *The Other Final*.

70. Mesut Ozil. He is of Turkish origin and has played for Real Madrid and Arsenal.

71. Ice hockey. Cech is the goaltender.

72. Amitabh Bachchan.

ROUND 10

Lionel Messi

73. Ronaldinho. They played together for Barcelona.

74. Sergio Ramos played 469 times for Real Madrid from 2005 to 2021 as a defender and 180 times for Spain. He plays for Paris Saint Germain as does Messi.

75. Robert Lewandowski of Poland. He was with Bayern Munich at that time.

76. Coach Mauricio Pochettino and players Angel di Maria and Leandro Paredes.

77. He scored five goals for Barcelona against Bayer Leverkusen in a 7-1 win in March 2012.

78. Socrates, captain of the 1982 Brazilian football team.

79. Diego Maradona.

80. Andres Iniesta, the midfielder who played 131 times for Spain and 442 times for Barcelona. He scored the winning goal in the dying moments of the 2010 World Cup final.

ANSWERS

ROUND 11

Cristiano Ronaldo

81. Luxembourg. They were his 113th, 114th, and his 115th international goals.

82. His baby son. He had unfortunately passed away just a few days earlier.

83. 30 years old

84. Ronaldo's side Manchester United lost 5-0 to Liverpool in October 2021. Mohammed Salah scored a hat-trick and a Ronaldo goal was disallowed because he was offside.

85. Coca-Cola.

86. Real Madrid, followed by Manchester United and Juventus.

87. Vogue Spain. Shayk and Ronaldo were on the cover and the accompanying headline was "Amor and Football (Love and Football).

88. Cod. It is a popular Portuguese dish.

ROUND 12

89. Osama bin Laden about 9/11. This is from the December 13, 2001 transcript of an Osama videotape.

90. Barcelona. This is because the Spanish Bourbon monarchy took over Barcelona (the city) in 1714.

91. Liston Colaco. The highest transfer amount till then was ₹ 80 lakh for Manvir Singh, from FC Goa to Mohun Bagan.

92. Harmanjot Singh Khabra, the star defender, and occasionally, a midfielder. He played for Chennaiyin and Bangalore in the Indian Super League before joining the Kerala Blasters.

93. Sadio Mane of Senegal. He is from Bambali, 400 km from Dakar, the capital of Senegal.

94. Marta Viera da Silva. She has been FIFA Women's World Player of the Year five times and runner-up four times.

95. Luis Figo (164 appearances for Real Madrid and 38 goals and 127 appearances for Portugal and 32 goals).

96. The Indian men's team.

ROUND 13

97. It is a dance move, based on his movements in the football field.

98. Paulo Maldini. He played 647 times for AC Milan and 126 times for Italy.

99. Pete Sampras, winner of 14 grand slams.

100. Arsenal.

101. *Dhan Dhana Dhan Goal (Get Set Goal)*, directed by Vivek Agnihotri.

102. Mohun Bagan.

103. This was after Paris Saint Germain advanced to the Champions League quarter-final with a 3-2 victory over Borussia Dortmund. In the first match of the two-leg tie, Erling Haaland had scored in a 2-1 win and had been photographed meditating after scoring a goal. In

Paris for the second leg, he had called Paris his city on Snapchat. Neymar's reply after the 2-0 victory was his Instagram post.

104. Alfredo de Stefano, who also had Spanish citizenship. He had won the Ballon d'Or earlier, in 1957 and 1959.

ROUND 14

105. None! The person with the highest number of red cards while playing for his country is Gerardo Bedoya of Colombia with 46.

106. Lev Yashin (1950-70) of the Soviet Union won, with Gordon Banks in second place and Dino Zoff in third place.

107. Vincent Kompany of Belgium, who played for 11 years for Manchester City.

108. His daughter, Ivy, was born with Down Syndrome. He also found that people like his daughter and their relatives had no one to speak for them.

109. Football!

110. Don Vito Corleone in *The Godfather*.

111. Atletico Madrid, one of the top three clubs in Spain, winning the La Liga more than ten times.

112. Neymar. Time, in February 2013, said he was the next Pele.

ROUND 15

113. Rivaldo in 1999, Ronaldinho in 2005 and Kaka in 2007.

114. Prasun Banerjee. He played for many years for Mohun Bagan and was elected to the Lok Sabha on a Trinamool Congress ticket.

115. Marco van Basten. He played 148 times for AC Milan, scoring 91 goals, and 48 times for The Netherlands, scoring 26. He played for Ajax and after retirement, managed The Netherlands.

116. Ronaldo de Lima of Brazil. He played 127 times for Real Madrid, scoring 83 goals, and 98 times for Brazil, scoring 68 goals.

117. Iker Casillas of Real Madrid and Spain. Gianluigi Buffon of Italy and Manuel Neuer of Germany have also won the award on five occasions.

118. Christian Vieri. He played 49 times for Italy, scoring 23 times.

119. Gisele Bündchen.

120. Cristiano Junior, playing for Dempo.

ROUND 16

121. Lionel Messi.

122. Pele and Diego Maradona. Pele won the FIFA magazine readers and experts poll with 72 per cent of the vote, di Stefano was second with 9 per cent, and Maradona third with 6 per cent. In the internet poll open to all, Maradona received 53 per cent of the vote and Pele got 18 per cent. Eusebio was third with 6 per cent.

123. Gerson de Oliviera Nunes. He played 87 times for Brazil, scoring 19 times. He played for Flamengo and Botafogo.

124. Luca Modric, who captained Croatia to the final of the 2018 World Cup. He has played for Real Madrid for years.

125. Romelu Lukaku of Belgium. He scored two goals in Belgium's 3-0 win over Russia.

126. It was Neymar's shirt. Neymar was injured in the quarter-finals against Colombia, but holding up the shirt was a way of saying that Neymar was present in spirit. It didn't help. Brazil lost 1-7 to Germany.

127. Andres Iniesta, the great Spanish midfielder. He played 442 times for Barcelona.

128. Sir Alex Ferguson, who coached Manchester United for 27 years.

ROUND 17

129. The bronze is called Headbutt. It shows Zinedine Zidane headbutting Marco Materazzi of Italy during the 2006 World Cup final between France and Italy. The referee red-carded Zidane and Italy won the match.

130. Brazil. Germany is next, with 226.

131. The International Federation of Football History and Statistics (IFFHS) has been awarding the World's Best Woman Goalkeeper Award since 2012. Hope Solo, an American, was the first winner. She has won the award four times.

132. Aditi Chauhan, the first woman to play for a major English club.

133. The film is the story of the kidnapping of di Stefano in Caracas in 1963, to draw attention to the misrule by the Venezuelan government. Kidnapped at gunpoint, he was not harmed and released without ransom after two days.

134. George Best. In that match, Manchester United defeated Benfica 5-1.

135. Roberto Baggio. He was voted Italian Player of the Century in 2000.

136. Goshto Pal. A defender, he was called The Great Wall of China.

ROUND 18

137. Gerd Muller. A phenomenal striker, he scored 398 goals in 453 matches for Bayern Munich and 68 goals in 62 matches for West Germany.

138. Spain.

139. Spain, Argentina and Colombia. He played 31 times for Spain, twice for Colombia and seven times for Argentina.

140. T. Asif Saheer. He captained Kerala in the Santosh Trophy.

141. Robert Lewandowski, the Polish captain. He has played for Bayern Munich and Barcelona.

142. Sepp Blatter, former FIFA president, banned from participating in football-related activities after reports about his role in some financial irregularities.

143. Paulo Maldini, one of the best defenders ever. He played all his life for AC Milan and 126 times for Italy.

144. Chuni Goswami, one of India's greatest footballers.

ROUND 19

145. Rafael Nadal. This was after Nadal won his 21st Grand Slam— the 2022 Australian Open. In his tweet, Godall referred to Nadal as Navidad. For, "Nadal" in Catalan means Christmas as does "Navidad" in Spanish.

146. Johan Cruyff, the Dutch captain in the 1974 World Cup. He was a great believer in "beautiful football."

147. Eusebio da Silva Ferreira. Originally from Mozambique, he played primarily for Benfica (317 goals in 301 matches) and Portugal (41 goals in 64 matches).

148. Edu or Eduardo Bedia, a Spaniard. A midfielder, he captained FC Goa.

149. Shyam Thapa. He mostly played for East Bengal and Mohun Bagan.

150. Jorginho or Jorge Luiz Frello Filho, the Brazilian born Italian midfielder.

151. Zlatan Ibrahimovic. He has played over 120 times for Sweden, scoring more than 60 goals and for top clubs like Paris Saint Germain, Juventus, AC Milan, Inter Milan and Barcelona.

152. Luca Modric, the Croatian midfielder who led his country to the World Cup final in 2018.

ROUND 20

153. Neil Armstrong and Edwin Aldrin landed on the Moon. Hazard would later wear the No. 7 jersey.

154. Arsenal. The 100th red card was given to Gabriel, the centre-back, in the match against Manchester United. His first yellow card was for dissent after Manchester United was awarded a penalty. The second was after he fouled Gabriel Jesus.

155. Miroslav Klose, a prolific scorer, including in World Cup tournaments. He has scored 16 goals, a record.

156. Paulo Maldini, the Italian defender and considered the best left-back in the history of football.

157. Sunil Chhetri, the Indian captain. He received the award in 2007, 2011, 2013, 2014, 2017 and 2018-19. He has played over 125 matches and scored more than 80 goals.

158. Naples, Italy. It is the home of Napoli, a club Maradona played 188 times for.

159. Gerd Muller for Bayern Munich and West Germany with 452 in the 70s and Hugo Sanchez for Atletico Madrid, Real Madrid and Mexico in the 80s with 315.

160. Romario with 340 goals for PSV Eindhoven, Barcelona, Flamengo, Valencia and Brazil in the 1990s.

Thierry Henry with 313 for Arsenal, Barcelona and France between 2000 and 2010.

ROUND 21

161. The Brazil-Italy match of 1982. "Beautiful" Brazil, needing a draw, lost 2-3 to "ugly" Italy.

162. Pep Guardiola, who coaches Manchester City and Dennis Bergkamp who worked at Ajax.

163. The Spain vs Holland final of 2010, the former winning through Andres Iniesta's goal. Seven Spaniards were associated with Johan Cruyff when they were at the La Masia, the Barcelona Youth Academy as were seven at the Ajax Youth Academy. Spanish players like Xavi, Iniesta, Sergio Busquets, Carlos Puyol and Gerard

Pique had worked with Johan Cruyff. So had Nigel de Jong, Wesley Sneijder, John Heitinga and others. Johan Cruyff supported Spain: they were truer to his style.

164. He wanted a tax cut. A highly paid player, he was in the highest tax-slab of 72 per cent.

165. Italy, and among the clubs, Bayern Munich and Manchester City.

166. Socrates, the Brazilian captain in 1982. He played 60 times for Brazil.

167. Barcelona, in 1996.

168. The Queen of Holland.

ROUND 22

169. Shakira, the Colombian singer.

170. Sadio Mane, the Senegalese forward. He has played nearly 100 times for Senegal and played 196 times for Klopp's Liverpool before moving to Bayern Munich.

171. To do something audacious or outrageously brilliant.

172. There is a photograph of his feet. For him, his feet brought him success. Ibrahimovic played over 120 times for Sweden, scoring 60 goals.

173. Kylian Mbappe of Paris Saint Germain and France, Mohammed Salah of Liverpool and Egypt and Raheem Sterling of Manchester City and England.

174. He meditates.

175. *Gladiator*. This is the mask worn by Maximus, the general, forced to become a gladiator by Emperor Commodus. Russell Crowe acts as Maximus.

176. Dani Alves. Both were defenders in the Barcelona side. Abidal played 76 games for Lyon and 125 for Barcelona, Alves over 250.

ROUND 23

177. Pope Francis, the head of the Roman Catholic Church.

178. Cafu (who has played 142 times as Brazil) as right back, Bobby Moore (108 caps for England) and Franz Beckenbauer (103 caps for West Germany) as the central defenders.

179. Diego Maradona (91 caps for Argentina), Zinedine Zidane (108 caps for France), Alfredo di Stefano (40 international caps for three countries) and Johan Cruyff (48 caps for Holland).

180. Robbie Fowler. He had reportedly said that the referee was either anti-English or anti-East Bengal. He was fined ₹ 5 lakh.

181. Brazil's 1970 side, with Pele, Tostao, Rivelino, Gerson, Jarzinho and Carlos Alberto.

182. Franco Baresi, Italian captain in 1994. He played 532 times for AC Milan.

183. Manuel Francisco dos Santos, or simply, Garrincha.

184. Mohammed or "Mo" Salah of Liverpool and Egypt.

ROUND 24

185. Capitalism! Barnes has said that creating a socialist society would destroy racism.

186. Paris Saint Germain. Lionel Messi, Kylian Mbappe and Neymar play for PSG.

187. Heineken's non-alcoholic beer.

188. Sergio Busquets, the Spanish captain.

189. Thierry Henry of Arsenal and 123 appearances for France. He is now one of the Belgian team's coaches.

190. The 1950 World Cup match with Uruguay. Brazil lost 1-2. If they had drawn the match, the World Cup would have been won.

191. The VAR or the video assistant referee

192. Marcus Rashford. He plays for Manchester United and England.

ROUND 25

193. David Beckham, the England captain. He played 115 times for the senior national side.

194. Eric Cantona. He became an actor.

195. Xavi Hernandes, one of the greatest midfielders. He played 133 times for Spain.

196. Chile.

197. All of them have won the World Cup both as player and manager. Zagallo won the World Cup in 1958 and 1962 as a player and in 1970 as a manager. Beckenbauer won the World Cup as a player in 1974 and as a manager in 1990. Didier Deschamps was part of the World Cup winning side in 1998 and was the manager in 2018 when France won the World Cup.

198. This was shortly after the Chernobyl nuclear disaster. Shevchenko lived in Kiev and was forced to move 1,000 km to the east after the disaster, the worst nuclear disaster ever. His mother was forced to burn the football as it had become radioactive.

199. Anirudh Thapa of Chennaiyin and India. He played 32 times for India, scoring three times.

200. Vicinius Junior. He has already begun playing for the Brazilian team.

ROUND 26

201. Brazil. Despite Kalyan's heroics, India lost 1-6 to Brazil.

202. The "d" stands for Dinho, her nickname and short for Ronaldinho.

203. Lilian Thuram. He was part of the French team that won the 1998 World Cup.

204. That China hosts the World Cup and third, wins the World Cup.

205. Zinedine Zidane. He played 108 times for France, scoring 31 goals. He coached Real Madrid.

206. Cricket. He spent a lot of time in Australia when he was young and played cricket there. He was an all-rounder and has a bat signed by Australian captain Allan Border.

207. Jurgen Klinsmann, part of the 1990 World Cup winning team. He played over a hundred times for his national team.

208. Francesco Totti. The only club he ever played for was Roma.

ROUND 27

209. George Best, Denis Law and Bobby Charlton.

210. It allowed players to take the knee and pay their respects to George Floyd, an African-American man killed by a policeman.

211. Spain's La Liga and Germany's Bundesliga.

212. Croatia, an important country in the football world. In the 2018 World Cup, Croatia had reached the final.

213. Borussia Dortmund.

214. Antony Matheus dos Santos or simply, Antony, a winger.

215. A "bread footballer" not only has to play well for himself, but for the club. Or simply, earn the club's bread.

216. Tibet. Bhutia said he sympathized with the Tibetan cause.

ROUND 28

Pele

217. Gordon Banks, the English goalkeeper with 73 international appearances. During a World Cup match with Brazil, he saved a certain goal by Pele.

218. He played the first half for New York Cosmos and the second, for Santos. These were the only two clubs he had ever played for.

219. Edson, his first name. Eventually, it was just "Pele."

220. The World Cup final of 1970. Brazil defeated Italy 4-1 and Pele opened the scoring.

221. Edinho is Pele's son. His full name is Edson Cholbi do Nascimento.

222. Russia's invasion of the Ukraine.

223. Pele joined New York Cosmos and football (or soccer as it's called there) well and truly came to the United States of America.

224. 15 centuries of fame!

ROUND 29

225. Jyoti Basu, chief minister of West Bengal, from 1977 to 2000.

226. Michael Jordan of the Chicago Bulls, the greatest basketball player ever.

227. Ronaldo, who led Brazil to World Cup victory in 2002.

228. Diego Maradona had just scored the "Hand of God" goal in the 1986 World Cup against England.

229. Jorge Valdano. He played 23 times for Argentina, scoring seven times.

230. The goal was against Belgium in the semi-finals of the 1986 World Cup. This was Maradona's second goal of the match, a solo effort.

231. Ephedrine. He was immediately banned.

232. Jorge Valdano, part of the 1986 World Cup winning team.

ROUND 30

233. Brazil. He played 505 times for Barcelona and 133 times for Spain.

234. Bayern Munich and Borussia Dortmund.

235. Paris Saint Germain and Olympique de Marseille.

236. Lionel Messi, who plays for Paris Saint Germain, a club Pochettino coaches.

237. Romeo Fernandes, for Atletico Paranaense, who won 5-0.

238. Virat Kohli, the former Indian captain.

239. Kylian Mbappe of Paris Saint Germain and France. He scored in the final of the 2018 World Cup, helping France to win 4-2.

240. Romario, a striker, with 55 goals in 70 appearances for Brazil.

ROUND 31

241. Robert Lewandowski, the Polish captain. After playing over 200 times for Bayern Munich, he has moved to Barcelona.

242. During the 2014 World Cup quarter-finals, he kneed Neymar in the back, damaging his spine and preventing him from playing in the semi-final against Germany. Brazil lost 1-7 and Zuniga apologized to Neymar, who accepted the apology.

243. Roberto Baggio, who played 56 times for Italy, scoring 27 goals.

244. Jorghino, the Italian defensive midfielder. He plays for Chelsea and Italy.

245. David Beckham. He played 115 times for England.

246. An orange!

247. Kuwait.

248. The trequartista attempts to dominate the midfield and moves ahead with the strikers. Diego Maradona was one and more recently, Ricardo Kaka.

ROUND 32

249. Pele had come with the Cosmos team to Kolkata in 1977. The match with Mohun Bagan ended in a 2-2 draw.

250. To Kylian Mbappe for scoring a goal in the 2018 World Cup final against Croatia. He was only the second teenager, after Pele, to do so.

251. Sachin Tendulkar, one of the world's all-time greats.

252. Karl-Heinz Rummenigge. Pele had said "Mr Rummenigge (who has won the Ballon d'Or twice) and ten robots."

253. Ronaldo. Besides playing 127 times for Real Madrid, a European club, he played 98 times for Brazil scoring 68 goals.

254. The Dutch team during the 2010 World Cup. It lost the final 0-1 to Spain.

ROUND 32

255. Gareth Southgate, the England team's manager.

256. Lothar Matthaus. He played 150 times for Germany or West Germany. Matthaus has given away both jerseys. Both are in museums.

257. Mahendra Singh Dhoni, one of India's most successful captains. He co-owns Chennaiyin FC.

258. Ederson Santana de Moraes of Brazil and Manchester City.

259. Divock Okoth Origi. The Serb basketballer is Vlade Divac. His father, Mike Origi, played for Kenya 48 times.

260. Andres Escobar, one of Colombia's star defenders. His own goal in the 1994 World Cup led to Colombia's elimination in the group stages. He was shot dead in Medellin, Colombia, a few days later.

ROUND 33

261. Paolo Rossi. He had admitted to being offered bribes, but not taking any. He played 48 times for Italy, scoring 20 goals.

262. Patrick Battiston. He had three cracked ribs, two broken teeth and damaged vertebrae. He was unconscious for a while. This was during the West Germany-France World Cup semifinal on 1982.

263. Harald “Toni” Schumacher, the West German goalkeeper. He played 76 times for the national side.

264. Son Hueng-min of South Korea. A speedy and skilled striker, he has scored over 30 times for his national side.

265. Ricardo Kaka. He played 92 times for Brazil, scoring 29 goals. He played regularly for AC Milan and Juventus.

266. Abedi Pele. His son, Andre Ayew, is the current captain of Ghana’s football team.

267. Uwe Seeler. He played for Hamburger SV.

268. Dino Zoff. He played for 15 years, retiring in 1983. He represented Italy 112 times.

269. Shane Warne, the Australian leg-spin bowler.

270. World War I. This happened in 1914, a few months after the war began and also, to an extent, in 1915.

271. Manipur. It was Manipur’s first Santosh Trophy triumph, defeating Kerala 2-1 in a closely-fought final.

272. Mohammedan Sporting. Hafiz Rashid and Saboo scored for Mohammedan Sporting. Among the spectators present was Mohammed Ali Jinnah, the father of the Pakistan nation.

ROUND 34

African Footballers

273. George Weah is the President of Liberia, since 2018. He played primarily for Monaco, Paris Saint Germain and AC Milan between 1988 and 2000 and for Liberia, 75 times.

274. Samuel Eto'o of Cameroon. He played 116 times for Cameroon, scoring 56 times.

275. Gabon, as a striker.

276. Romelu Lukaku. He plays for Inter-Milan and having already played over a hundred times for the national team and scored 68 times.

277. Ivory Coast.

278. Zambia.

279. Nigeria.

280. Ivory Coast. He has played 30 times, so far.

ROUND 36

281. The Davis Cup, a major tennis tournament.

282. Norway.

283. Flow Kingz is an amateur pop group.

284. Lionel Messi.

285. The price of fish in Kolkata goes up and down depending who wins. If East Bengal wins, the price of the Hilsa, associated with the club, goes up. If East Bengal loses, Hilsa prices go down.

286. The academies thought he was too small to be a footballer. He moved to Spain after that.

287. Bobby Moore, just before the 1970 World Cup. It was found that there was no truth in the allegations.

288. Kevin de Bruyne, one of Belgium's best players. He's played a hundred times for his national side and also, represents Manchester City.

ROUND 37

289. Jean-Paul Sartre. Awarded the Nobel in 1964, he declined.

290. Anil Kapoor. Amrita Singh, Raakhee and Utpal Dutt arc thc othcr big stars in thc film.

291. Gareth Bale, who has also played for Real Madrid.

292. Robert Firmino. He also plays for Liverpool.

293. Gary Linekar. He played for England in the 1980s.

294. Nigeria, three-time Africa Cup of Nations winners.

295. Cristiano Ronaldo and Lionel Messi.

296. I.M. Vijayan. He played 71 times for India, scoring 32 times.

ROUND 38

297. They are all clothing brands.

298. Eric Cantona. He played 45 times for France, scoring 20 goals.

299. Australia. The men's team has won the AFC Asian Cup

300. Alisson, the goalkeeper. He had left his goal to come to the West Brom penalty area. He headed home. It was the first field goal by a Liverpool goalkeeper, ever.

301. Neymar, Lionel Messi and Kylian Mbappe. All of them are at Paris Saint Germain. He said Neymar needs to have the ball and feel the ball. Mbappe needs space and high tempo. Messi needs another tempo.

302. Chile.

303. Japan. The tsunami leading to the problem at the Fukushima nuclear power plant.

304. Majid Bishkar played for East Bengal and then, for Mohammedan Sporting as a midfielder or forward along with Jamshed Nassiri.

ROUND 39

305. The Jules Rimet Trophy, awarded to the winner of the World Cup, was stolen just before the tournament began. Pickles, quite fortuitously, found it.

306. After Brazil won the 1970 tournament, the trophy went permanently to Brazil, according to the rules. The trophy was stolen in 1983 and though people were arrested, it was never recovered.

307. Gerard Piqué. He has played 397 times for Barcelona and before that 22 times for Real Zaragoza.

308. Marco van Basten, with 24 goals in 58 matches for Holland and 219 goals in 281 club games.

309. Mohammed Habib. He was part of the team that won the bronze medal in the 1970 Asian Games.

310. This was an unbelievable match with an unexpected result. Germany defeated Brazil 7-1 in the World Cup semi-final. All of them scored, Kroos and Schurrle twice.

311. Ferenc Puskas, the Hungarian "Galloping Major."

312. Franco Baresi. He played 532 times for AC Milan and 81 times for Italy as a central defender.

ROUND 40

313. Silvio Berlusconi, later Prime Minister of Italy for many years.

314. Nasser was the referee when Maradona scored the Hand of God goal. He allowed the goal, when it clearly wasn't one. It ensured a 2-1 victory for Argentina over England in the 1986 World Cup.

315. Bob Houghton, from England. He served between 2006 and 2011.

316. Italy. The game became very defensive.

317. Greece. As Konstantis Karamanlis, then Prime Minister, said: "Greece is on the lips of everyone in the world who follows this mass and magical sport called football."

318. Dempo Sports Club.

319. Cuban leader Fidel Castro.

320. Pele.